June, 1995

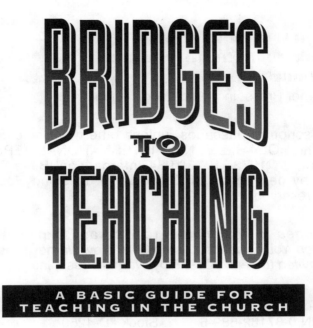

A BASIC GUIDE FOR TEACHING IN THE CHURCH

Kenneth F. Hall

Warner Press, Inc.
Anderson, Indiana

Bridges to Teaching:
A Basic Guide for Teaching in the Church
by Kenneth F. Hall
Warner Press, Inc. Anderson, Indiana

Bridges to Teaching is revised and expanded from *Develop Your Talent to Teach* ©1977 by Warner Press, Inc., and *Invited to Teach* ©1988 by Warner Press, Inc.

Copyright ©1995 by Warner Press, Inc.
ISBN 0-87162-689-6   Stock #D-4250
UPC #730817211466
All Rights Reserved
Printed in the United States of America

Eidtor in Chief: David C. Shultz
Book Editor: Dan Harman
Cover by Larry Lawson

Finding Your Way through This Book

Foreword

This is a book about the good news—the gospel of Jesus Christ. This is a book about persons—who they are and what they need. This is a book about teaching—helping persons to perceive the gospel, to accept the gospel, and to fulfill the gospel.

At some point in every junior-level Sunday school curriculum the question is asked, "What is the gospel?" The usual answer has always been, "The good news." This book goes beyond the "usual answers" and helps both the experienced teacher and the prospective teacher to understand that the gospel is the good news that God is in Christ, reconciling the world unto himself. Ken Hall then helps us to understand how to teach effectively.

One could ask, "What does it mean to "teach"? This book helps us to see that the more appropriate question is "What does it mean to teach the gospel to persons?" Persons, whether they are six, sixteen, or sixty, ask three questions—"Who am I?" "Who are you?" and "What is the world all about?" Ken Hall shows us how to help persons whom we teach to find the answers to these questions in light of the gospel.

The author has his roots in the best of Christian education past and is on the growing edge of current insights into teaching persons. He lifts up the importance of "relational teaching," of the "story" and "narrative" approaches to theology and methodology. The book brings to us new insights into learner preferences and learning styles. Where curriculum resources use uniform themes the book brings helpful understandings of what this means to age-level distinctives.

Ken Hall is a master teacher. He is a master writer. To the task of helping us to be more effective teachers he brings a rich background—husband, father, teacher, curriculum developer and writer, book editor, Christian education professor.

I have known him for a long time. He has always helped me to believe in the teaching church and to find joy in teaching. I think you will find it as well.

Sherrill D. Hayes
Executive Director
Board of Christian Education of the Church of God

Therefore go and make disciples of all nations, baptizing them in the name of the Father and of the Son and of the Holy Spirit, and teaching them to obey everything I have commanded you.

—Matthew 28:19–20

Chapter 1

Bridges to Good Teaching

- *What is good teaching, anyway?*
- *Don't you have to be a "born teacher"?*
- *What gifts for teaching do I have?*
- *Should I teach in the church this coming year?*

The Brooklyn Bridge. One of the wonders of the world when it was built. Supposedly sold a thousand times to rubes visiting New York City. There's something fascinating about bridges. Romantic covered bridges on country roads. How glorious to watch the sun set behind the Golden Gate Bridge! Don't suppose you ever thought about building a bridge, did you? If you have no more engineering and construction skills than I have, you probably wouldn't give it much thought.

Yet there is something within us that calls us to bridge-building. And we may have actually built more bridges than we realize. After all, much of the Christian life is about bridge-building. We are called to link ourselves with fellow Christians. We are invited to reach out to people in need. In various ways we are called to teach, and that is a bridge-building undertaking. We shall explore the meaning of that across the coming pages.

Teachers are very much needed as bridge-builders in the church. They help to link their learners with each other and with God. They bring together Bible and life. They encourage growing persons to stretch into a significant future with Christ as their leader.

Let's eavesdrop now on a conversation in which some interesting questions are being raised about being a bridge-building teacher:

"Well, John and Ginny, you've been worshiping with us for about a year now, haven't you?" Pastor Hale asked as he sat with the young couple in their living room over cups of coffee. They nodded, recognizing that he and Mrs. Jenkins, the Sunday school director in their church, had come here for a special reason, and now they were getting to it.

"I like the way you've become involved in activities around the church," said Mrs. Jenkins. "You seem to be growing persons."

"Did you ever teach a class in your church back in Centerton?" the pastor wanted to know.

"Well, no, we never did." But Ginny looked at John. "You did help with the youth one year, didn't you?"

"That was about five years ago," John agreed. "Had a good time. But I've never thought of myself as a teacher. Ginny gets the credit for teaching our kids a few things. I like to get my hands into practical things."

"Well, I've noticed you have been very faithful in a lot of service activities and in Bible study," said Pastor Hale. "That gave me a clue that you might like to teach."

Ginny chimed in. "I do think that John is more of a teacher than he realizes. He certainly is a good role model for our children. And he's taught us all a lot in direct ways, too."

By now John was looking a bit puzzled. "Don't you have to be called in order to do things around the church? I'm not sure that I've ever been called. And then maybe I'm just looking for an excuse."

"I don't know about that," said Ginny, "but I'd say that all of us Christians have been asked to help spread the gospel and to support the growth and nurture of our fellow Christians."

"I agree with that," said the pastor, "and I'd also say that the two of you show evidence of being called to be teachers. For one thing you seem to have the gifts that go with it."

"What in the world are you talking about?" John wanted to know.

"Well you seem to have some of the gifts Paul writes about. I see particularly in both of you a gift for discernment, for example. You have good insights into the faith. And there are other things I see in you both as well. You can express yourselves. You have a deep and abiding love for the Lord and for people. You are dependable. You seem to build bridges between people and between God and them. You have the message of the gospel that you demonstrate in your own lives and can share."

"Part of the picture," said Mrs. Jenkins, "is also that we have a real need of your help with our upper elementary children this fall and you can help meet it. So we are coming to you and inviting you to jump in."

"Think about it," said Pastor Hale, "We're inviting you to the ministry of teaching. Pray about it. Do you sense the need? Do you feel the support of our congregation in accepting the invitation? How are you qualified to answer it? What more can you do to give yourself to it? Consider the gifts the Lord has given you and the general commission we all share to go into the world and teach the gospel."

We can sum up the need this way:

Bridge-Building Teachers Wanted—For some of the most important work in the world, men and women not necessarily highly trained but willing to work at the job. Not necessarily skilled in human relations but with warm and loving hearts and a desire to get to know people better. Growing as Christians and in knowledge of the faith.

Not having all the time in the world but willing to find time for adequate preparation, time to get to know students through the week. No salaries, but opportunities for rich rewards in personal satisfaction, friendship, and a sense of service. Apply to your pastor or Christian education leader to be a teacher in the work of the church. Openings for qualified persons at all age levels.

What Is the Need for Teachers?

Almost everybody wants to teach somebody something. We started off young. When our little sister scribbled on our favorite book, we yelled, "I'll teach you to do that to my book!" and then we proceeded to teach that somebody something. We've been teaching people things ever since by intent or by accident. Brothers and sisters teach each other—about family and neighborhood customs. They may not always set out to teach, but they share nevertheless in the highly important process of teaching by socialization.

In that process one person catches from those around something about how to live life through customs and common practices and attitudes that are encountered. Parents teach their children, usually through a mixture of a little intentional teaching and a lot of indirect example.

What little I eventually learned about golf, fishing, hunting, and a number of other skills, I picked up from neighbors who happened to know about some things my parents—all-wise as I sometimes thought they were—didn't know.

And the church always has need for teachers. This involves youth leaders who use the skills of teaching. Leaders of Scout groups. Men and women's groups who teach as they lead. And teachers in the Sunday school. Most churches are trying to fill vacancies for one-fourth to one-third of their staff each fall. Emergencies are always arising that call for more people who can teach. There are never enough teachers.

Kinds of Teachers

People who teach don't all look and act alike. They have different attributes to bring to the job and different tendencies in their teaching. Some of these attributes are more helpful than others.

4

Some of their approaches are of more significance than others. We are about to survey some common styles of teaching. As you read through these, consider which are most important for teaching as you understand what that role should be.

The Performer

These teachers have a flair for dramatics and know how to put on a good show. They get a kick out of entertaining people and feel with good reason that to build a class and keep its interest, there is need to provide some kind of entertainment.

Such teachers are interested in showy methods. They like to stay in the limelight. They seek to develop strong attachments between themselves and students, particularly since those will feed into their own egos. For them, the teaching-learning process consists of a flashy, attention-demanding way of presenting information to the students. There are some good things about this approach, of course. It is good to try to keep students interested and involved.

The Scholar and Question-Answerer

These teachers most frequently find their way into youth and adult levels of teaching. Often such persons are knowledgeable and have much to share. Sometimes, however, such teachers don't really know as much as they think they do. At any rate, the class session resembles a university lecture hall where the renowned Doctor So-and-So presents a famous lecture and then patiently answers questions for a few minutes at the end. These teachers generally prepare well and may have a good style of presentation. Where students are not highly motivated from within or where they need help in thinking or working things through, this approach poses problems in the church school.

The Director-Disciplinarian

Having an orderly and efficiently run classroom is important to such teachers. They run things with the style of a top sergeant. These teachers allow little informal activity in their rooms. They have firmly in mind what they want to teach, and they are going to teach it no matter what! No talking back. No freewheeling exploring and discovering. The plan for the class will be followed precisely, or they'll know the reason why. Such efficiency has its value, but often more learning takes place in an informal, relaxed setting.

Student among Students

Teachers like this are eager to learn. They see themselves as having as much to learn as any of the students and decide that they will learn alongside them. They will explore together. They will work on projects together. Of course, they study in advance and learn more than the students most of the time, but they see themselves as full members of the learning community. They will set the pace for learning; their learning will serve as an inspiration to the students. They will sense their fellowship together. Sometimes in their learning alongside students they may not be far enough out in front of them to help them move along efficiently or to provide them with the fullest resources for learning.

The Resource Provider

Materials, audiovisuals, study aids, resource packets, books—such teachers know what the sources of information are for their class and where they can be found. These leaders are librarians and collectors. They have a nose for all kinds of learning helps. They may particularly like to use learning centers in which materials are to be used, books are to be read, records are to be listened to, and learning games are to be played. They recognize that students must take much responsibility for their own learning and feel that a good way to encourage that is to keep bringing in all kinds of materials to help them.

The Friend and Guide

These teachers see themselves as brothers or sisters who know something about finding their way along the Christian path. With more experience and more study in their background than many of the students, they can point the way over familiar ground to those who are less experienced. They can help them know all the alternatives. The friend and guide types of teacher can provide experiences and materials drawn from their background. They are not different kinds of persons from the students; they are one with them but with the assignment to provide leadership and to carry on planning.

Rather than dictating what should happen in the classroom, these persons bring up the possibilities. They have at hand a variety of aids for classroom process. They are friendly, concerned, caring, and sharing.

The Story-Teller

These teachers know the Story and the stories about how God has dealt with his people, and they are able in narrative style to share these accounts with their students. They are able to guide and stimulate the learners to identify with and participate in the stories in an active way. They do not use stories simply to illustrate the points they wish to make but see the gospel story, for example, as central to all that is taught, all that the Christian believes. They have a good feel for what makes a story interesting and the mechanics for telling it convincingly. They believe that much of what people learn is best supported by narrative.

The Encourager

Such a teacher believes that learning happens best when the student is properly supported, believed in, stimulated to accomplish. Such a teacher will spend time in prayer for the students. This teacher will send notes of support frequently and will pass along honest compliments. This teacher will find time to be with the students through the week and in other activities in which they are involved. In class the teacher is sensitive not to hurt or put down anyone.

Putting the Best Qualities Together

We have just been looking at some common types of teachers. Most of us have some tendencies in each of these directions. Most of us also might more easily see ourselves in one role than another. Indeed our thoughts of what a teacher should be might turn toward one or several of these models. In identifying some of the best qualities, we can look to the performer type with appreciation for the desire to be interesting and to attract learners to the process. We are indebted to all teachers who perform well.

We can model ourselves in some respects after the scholar who takes the subject matter seriously, who learns and shares freely. But we don't have to be advanced scholars to serve well as teachers. It is important to have the qualities of the friend and guide to go with that. It is good if we feel the need to keep on learning ourselves. It is good if we encourage the students to be active in the class, in planning it and carrying it out.

One advantage in being an inexperienced teacher is that we can more readily decide on what model of teacher we will work at becoming. We can build bridges between the best in all these teaching roles so that they can operate together through us in the classroom. The teachers we have known who have been most genuinely effective in the long range can serve as our examples. But even the most experienced teachers can shift gears if they are dissatisfied with how they are doing now. Considering how very important teaching is, we are probably always going to be hungry to broaden and deepen our skills in these varying roles.

Another way of bridging to these varying skills is to be involved with others in team teaching. One member of the team may be more of an encourager, another more of managing director. One may be the scholar, another the storyteller. Sometimes a wife and husband team may work well at this, but even more frequently this may be another pair of persons who determine that their particular skills complement each other.

What Are Your Talents for Teaching?

Of course, some people simply weren't born to be teachers. But about everybody can develop more skills in this area, and in the process they may become very effective teachers in the church's classrooms. Other aspects of their lives may also serve. So many of the vocations we follow can add to our talent to teach. In most of our jobs we have occasion to teach new persons or to train others in aspects of our work. Parents are called upon to act as teachers for their children. Most of us have some general gifts that at least put us on the road toward being good teachers.

Anyone able to read this text has the ability to learn and to grow. God planned for all of us to grow. And as we grow we can develop into more of the kind of teacher we would like to be. As we consider what alterations we can make in our lives, we can move in the direction of greater teaching skills and sensitivities. As we go through our own processes for learning and growth, we learn well the kinds of struggles and hopes of those who would learn with our help.

We also teach by the kind of person we are. Our basic, underlying life commitments speak loudly in any ongoing class relationship. Our commitment to Christ, the priorities we give to his work, the consistency of our ethics, our love for God, for the written Word, and for the church—these all show themselves to our students apart from the words we say. Students can read hypocrisy and inconsistency fast. Our genuineness can be read, and it teaches.

How much we really care about other people shows up as we go about our teaching responsibilities. We teach about love by the way we live a life of loving concern. Our compassion and our goodwill come across to people, and students may imitate them.

We have varied backgrounds and characteristics that can contribute to teaching. Some of us have a wealth of knowledge and experience out of which to share. The rest of us are building up that store. Some of us have developed skill in really listening to other persons, in drawing them out so that they can share their innermost thoughts. We may have learned something about informal counseling. This can contribute to our teaching.

Some of us are like Yellowstone National Park's Old Faithful. We can be depended upon. That attitude itself can communicate a spirit of dedication, concern, and caring that says more than words. It says to learners that the teacher thinks they and their learning activities are important and are worth being kept high on a priority list. Steadiness, promptness, keeping one's word, living according to priorities all are learnings that are communicated through life. In surveys of what learners expect of their leaders, dependability is a virtue that ranks high with them.

Some teachers bring other qualities that make special contributions to teaching. Some are very creative persons as they begin their teaching. They know how to take elements that are given to them and combine these into something new and fresh. They are always uncovering different possibilities in teaching. They allow God, who makes all things new, to exercise creativity through them. Others learn how to apply useful creativity to their teaching to bring it freshness as they go along. They bridge between the new and the old to create something marvelous in the classroom.

Some of us are dreamers. We can imagine things as they ought to be, as they might be. We have a highly developed sense of idealism. We can envision the possibilities for the future through different ways of doing things now. We can dream dreams for our students, our classes, our congregation. The quality of dreaming good things can go hand in hand with teaching.

Most of us have special hobbies, skills, and interests. A photographer's skills can be used in taking photos, slides, or videos and in helping class members use photography for learning activities. The teacher who loves to read can share stories, information, and ideas from a storehouse of books. The collector can bring in items that relate to the class. The dressmaker or tailor might help with costumes. The traveler can share stories, pictures, and curios from far-away places.

Some of us feel more like followers than leaders. We may feel more comfortable behind the spotlight than under it. Others of us may feel most comfortable in shared leadership roles and in a mixture of following and leading. The teacher frequently turns the leadership role over to students as they plan, bring reports, take initiative in the class. There are the shared leadership roles of team teachers. Teachers who feel that they must be always and forever leading in a strongly directive style are handicapped as enablers of learning.

Picture Yourself in the Classroom

Whether or not you have ever taught a class, no matter your experience or inexperience, you may have some picture of yourself as a teacher. You may envision yourself standing in front of rows of people. You may see yourself with a message of great importance burning on your heart that you desire to share. You may picture yourself walking into a classroom with fear and trembling, carrying out your duty. You may even imagine yourself receiving admiration and praise from students.

Actually, any picture of yourself in the classroom should be surrounded by visions of quite a bit of time in other classes preparing to teach and sharpening teaching skills. It will include time spent in person-to-person contact with students and their families. It will include preparation during the week—study of the Bible for next week's session as a part of personal devotional life, session planning, and background reading.

Then into the classroom itself you go. There you will be following one of, or some combination of, the roles described under "Look at Some Different Kinds of Teachers." You will be describing how to do interesting things, modeling a significant Christian life in personal contacts in the classroom.

Some of the time you will be presenting things in an interesting manner to the total group. At other times you will be working with small groups, committees, or individuals. A lot of time will be spent encouraging students in their own leadership roles in the class. Part will be spent helping them to form and clarify their values and to build up significant Christian commitment. Answers to questions and problems will not come too quickly; instead students will be encouraged to explore issues and reach answers of their own, checking them out with the word that comes from Christ. Frequently you will be asking simply, "Why?"

As a growing teacher you will find a variety of ways of providing the necessary content for a session. This will include learning the most appropriate resources. You will know the general curriculum plan of which your teaching is a part and will seek diligently to fit into its flow for the most desirable sequence, balance, and comprehensiveness. At the same time through bridging between the gospel and current life concerns you will stay relevant to student need.

Often you will be working as a member of a teaching team. You will share in this work with another teacher or teachers in your classroom, and you will be coordinating with other teachers in your department and throughout the Sunday church school. You will keep in touch with parents and other members of your students' families. It all is a good and worthy dream, and it can come true.

TEACHING ON THE AGE LEVELS

Notes to Teachers of Young Children

Am I qualified to be a teacher of young children? Teaching at this level should not be left to any one small category of persons—young women, jolly Aunt Marys, new converts, high school youth. A distinguished seminary professor of theology deliberately chose five-year-olds as the age he would teach in the church school, saying "These children ask all the profound questions, and it calls for all the skill I can develop to deal with them."

The senior pastor of a large congregation and his wife taught the two-year-olds in their church. Along with having a wonderful ministry with the children themselves, they became closely acquainted with the young families in their church. A church teaching staff for young children is blessed if it can have teachers, both men and women, younger and older, with varying experiences in the Christian faith to model.

Some especially desirable qualities to share are these: an imagination to accompany the growing capacity for fantasy these young children have; a recognition of the importance of play in the child's learning processes and an ability to play along with the children; a sensitivity to the differences among individual children; an awareness of the brevity of their attention span; patience and the capacity to adjust to the varying moods of children from day to day; a skill in relating to children meaningfully in their life together and in light of the gospel.

Studying this chapter in light of early childhood: Make a job description for the kind of person you feel would best serve as a teacher of children ages two through five. What qualities would you rate most highly? How would you apply the general qualities of being a teacher to the ministry with these youngest persons?

Notes to Teachers of Elementary Children

What a range of exciting new learning possibilities there are in the children you teach! New and growing skills in reading. New abilities to comprehend and put together information from the Bible and the world around. Almost untapped capacity to remember. At the same time this child across these elementary years is most skilled at concrete, factual thinking rather than thinking in the abstract. That provides an interesting challenge to the teacher.

These are great times for hero worship, for listening and sharing stories of the faith. Teachers with ability to tell stories, to guide children on the high energy level with which they can approach learning are in special demand in the church. Teachers who can make sound use both of a small bit of competition and a large dose of cooperation in group process are needed. Teachers who can help harness the energy of these years for effective learning and life change are called for.

Studying this chapter in light of elementary childhood: Make a job description for the kind of person you feel would best serve in the church as a teacher of children in grades one to six. What qualities would you rate most highly? How would you apply the specific qualities of being a teacher to the teaching of children at this particular age?

Notes to Teachers of Youth

What kind of person is most likely to teach young people effectively? Here we are trying to relate the gospel to adolescents who at one moment seem like children and at another moment like adults. Here we are with some being tossed by the tempestuous times that go with moving into adulthood. Here we are with some who are in rebellion against parents, church, and the society around them. Others seem not at all affected by that. All are putting priority on conforming to a teen society of peers rather than conforming to adult expectations.

The teacher of youth does generally need a fair degree of energy. The teacher needs to know who she or he is quite clearly as a basis for modeling good self-identity with youth. The teacher needs to come at this ministry with a spirit of openness and flexibility while clearly representing the church in its ministry. Young people them-selves indicate in survey after survey that a big thing they look for in adult youth leaders more than glamour or flashiness is depend-ability and stability, a person they can count on.

An adult is needed here that the youth can relate to and model after, an adult who has gone along this pathway before them with some clarity and success.

Here is an adult who is a vital Christian, not stuffy but not shal-low either, serious but with a good sense of humor. That is an inter-esting combination to put together, isn't it?

Studying this chapter in light of youth: Make a job description of the kind of person who would best serve the church as a teacher of its youth from about grade seven through twelve. What qualities would you rate most highly? How would you apply the general qualities that go with being a teacher to the ministry of teaching youth?

Notes to Teacher of Adults

Many teachers find the most personal satisfaction in all that they do by teaching a class of adults. Those class members can be high-ly appreciative and highly flattering. And indeed it does help to receive such feedback. It is good to find that adults can show appreciation and support for their teachers and that they can also provide some honest feedback about what makes for effective teaching. Most teachers of adults will find themselves being most effective when they are able to bring insights from the Bible to bear on relevant life situations, varied as those are, among their particu-lar adult students.

This will usually involve a great deal of discussion. A key skill for an adult teacher is to be an effective discussion leader, identify-ing key issues, helping the class to deal systematically with the issues, and making clear progress as the class moves past pooling ignorance to achieving new insights and making significant com-mitments for change together.

Woe be to that teacher who simply turns his or her class into another little church service within the church and provides a sec-ond sermon for the morning. The church has an opportunity to approach adults in varying rich and significant ways when there is a marked difference between the proclamation and devotion of the worship hour and the mind-expanding exploration of the class period.

Studying this chapter in light of adulthood: Make a job description of the kind of person who would best serve the church as a teacher of adults. Consider any differences you might see between teaching a general class of all ages and kinds of adults or classes divided among younger, middle, and older adults or divided by life interest groups. What qualities would rate most highly? How would you modify the general good qualities of teaching for use in the ministry of teaching adults?

STUDYING THIS CHAPTER IN CLASS

Possible Goals
• To survey the need for teachers in the church and consider the possibility of answering a call to teach.

• To understand the qualities that go into teaching at its best.

• To take an inventory of personal talents for teaching.

A Class Plan
1. Introduce the course.

2. Survey the need for qualified teachers in the church's educational ministry.

3. Set priorities on the qualities most needed in teaching. (On separate 8½ by-11-inch sheets of paper write from the text some of the terms used for teaching: The Performer, Scholar, Question-Answerer, Director-Disciplinarian, Student among Students, Resource Provider, Friend and Guide, Story Teller, Encourager. You might add other possible titles such as Coach, Inspirer, Listener. Discuss the meaning of each title and ask the students arrange the sheets in the order of importance that they would assign to them.)

4. Define good teaching. (Draw on class discussion and the text to define what good teaching involves the most—emphasizing material under "Putting the Best Qualities Together.")

5. Consider what talents members of the group have for teaching. (Ask students to write talents they regard as important for teaching on a sheet of paper. Gather these up and redistribute them to students so that they will not easily know whose sheet they have. Share these with appreciation and consider what contribution each varied talent can make to teaching. See "What Are Your Talents for Teaching?")

6. Sum up: Define teaching. (Consider what most people have to bring to teaching and what they need to learn.)

Your hands made me and formed me;
give me understanding to learn your commands.
—Psalm 119:73

Chapter 2

Bridges to the Persons We Teach

Who are these people I am supposed to teach?

How do people grow? Can I help or hinder?

How can we know people as individuals not clustered into stereotypes?

How can I relate better to the people I teach?

A huddle group at a Christian education workshop were getting acquainted. They were talking about who and what they taught back home.

"I teach the Bible," said one.

"I teach Christ."

"I teach the Christian faith."

"I teach our church curriculum."

"Well, I teach children."

Note the range of answers around this circle.

Certainly we do generally teach a content. (That will be the subject of another chapter in this book.) Certainly we do carry a high concern to teach the Bible, its backgrounds, its story, its precepts. Of couse, it is always helpful to teach in accordance with a good curriculum plan. These factors are foundational.

At the same time it is important to remember that we teach people. Our teaching process is not complete if we focus only on its content. Our responsibility is to bridge between the Bible and other significant content and persons. The teaching process lacks point and significance if ultimately we are not teaching persons in relation to the biblical concepts and the gospel insights and the daily life understandings that are so important.

The people we teach come in all shapes, sizes, ages, and conditions. While groups of learners have much in common, depending on their age and background, they remain individuals, each one created by God as a unique and worthy person. They relate to each other, to teachers, and to learning in different ways. Thus it can make for an interesting time when a group of people get together in a class with one or two teachers to do some learning. The mood and style of a class can vary not only because of the different personalities involved but also because of changing moods, subject matter, weather, and what happened on the way to Sunday school.

This creates a particular problem for a teacher who depends upon printed curriculum resources to supply an unfailing lesson plan to fit her or his unique situation.

More than a hundred years ago some of the pioneer Sunday school planners had the dream of plotting out a common lesson for everybody in the church to study at the same time on Sunday morning. Oh, the students might move into separate classes according to age and perhaps to sex. But they could all on their own terms study a common Bible passage and a central idea for the day.

As the years wore on, many teachers became more and more concerned that they couldn't begin to deal with the same ideas with a five-year-old that they were facing with a seventeen-year-old. Interests, learning capacities, background, and development all varied too much.

This led eventually to some of the churches setting up closely graded classes (and publishing supporting teaching resources) that would make a distinction between a third grader and a fourth grader. But the fact remains that sometimes the differences between two third graders is greater than between a second grader and a fourth grader. The most common solution from a curriculum planning standpoint these days is for courses to be planned on a group basis of two or three grades. Such planning tries to be in the ballpark with the common developmental needs of children.

The result is that teachers are called upon to adapt resources, session plans, everything from a given curriculum series to the special and individual needs of their students. This is true no matter how specific and detailed is the guidance provided by a set of curriculum materials. When materials put all the words in the teacher's mouth, they are on the surface making it easier for that teacher. But in reality they are making the work of that teacher to relate closely and directly to the situation of each student all the more difficult.

Learners need to be approached in many different kinds of ways. Sometimes they need to relate one to one with a wise and open teacher or leader. Often they can do some learning on their own through learning centers. More often they will learn most effectively by studying in classes of peer groups at which a sensitive teacher is present to assist the group in its exploring and discovering. At other times they may gain the most from intergenerational experiences in which a grandfather relates to a young adult or a teenager relates to a six-year-old. All of these approaches can be joined to support a learning community. Drawing from one source here and another source there, in structured class settings or in informal family and peer group relationships, through the worship services of the church—this all adds up to learning in the Christian community.

The teacher is usually concerned with a school type of setting and how to assist students in learning there. But the dedicated teacher will understand how all these other home and church settings add up to a unity in nurturing of the learner.

Look at Some Learners

In order to work at our understandings of how to relate to individuals as teachers and as members of the Christian community interested in the learning process, let's look at some individuals and consider how the teacher may best relate to them and support them in the learning process.

Karen

Karen is a bright and attractive four-year-old. She knows the rudiments of adding. She recognizes letters and associates them with sounds. She is on the verge of reading, but her parents do not want to push her in that direction. She thinks in very imaginative ways. She has been taken to church ever since she was a baby and thinks of her Sunday school room as a happy place she looks forward to being in whenever she can. "That's my church," she sometimes says proudly when the family drives by their church building during the week.

She has heard and loves many stories of Jesus, although she does not of course understand much about his having lived long ago in a faraway country. She has heard about God being Jesus' father and thinks God must be like the angels she has seen pictured, but her notions are foggy. She knows her mother and father love her and that is how she interprets people loving her at church and Jesus loving her. She has a short attention span. Her main occupation in life is playing. She wants to please her parents and avoid their anger. She likes to be praised when she has done something good and to receive attention and rewards.

Randy

A rambunctious second-grader, Randy is full of life and mischief. He usually has a twinkle in his eye, even when he's in trouble and knows it. Randy is being raised by his mother along with four brothers and sisters. He can barely remember his dad. His mother has a rough life and is away from her family at her job most of the time. Randy has been coming to church now for a year. He hasn't always known how to be accepted at this church. The other children have been there longer than he, and their parents are active in the church. He is sometimes regarded as a discipline problem. So far he has responded most favorably to praise for good behavior. He has been reprimanded repeatedly for misbehavior. His teacher has reported his poor behavior to his mother, and she has punished him for acting poorly at church. He is pretty much controlled by "What's in it for me?" He wants his way, he wants attention, and he'll get away with whatever he can. He has made rather slow progress in school and has little backing at home for what he is learning. He is on a first-grade reading level, whereas some of the children in his Sunday school class are reading at third and fourth grade levels.

Mike

Mike is an earnest fourth-grader. He doesn't always perform very well. Mike is not the brightest child around, but he almost always works hard at things. He's dependable, cooperative, conscientious. He goes by the book. If the school rules say that he must not do something, he obeys that rule without question. He tries to put into practice the rules he learns at church that come out of the Bible. He's very literalistic about these, very legalistic. He hasn't thought through the rules he lives by, but he is devoted to them. He has heard that children should give themselves to Jesus Christ, and so he has bowed at an altar and done that to the best of his ability. He has heard at his church that those who have given themselves to Jesus should then be baptized, and he has asked about this, but has been discouraged from doing it at his age. He wants to please people and he wants to feel that he belongs wherever he goes.

A very concrete thinker, Mike really is not able to understand symbolic acts. He is a fairly accomplished reader, and he reads his Bible regularly. He likes doing that, feels good about it. He has perfect attendance this year at church and at school. Mike enjoys good health and has a quiet, pleasant personality. He gets along better with adults than with children his age. He feels safer with adults and better liked by them than by most children of his age.

Sherry

An eighth-grader, Sherry is a bubbly thirteen-year-old who is quite aware of being a new teenager. She moves from a teenage sophistication to a childlike girlhood as quickly as she can move from playing with a doll in her room to talk about boys over the phone with her girl friend. She is coming to terms with her adolescent body, looks to be at least sixteen even when acting like a ten-year-old. She sometimes fusses with her parents, particularly her mother whom she feels restricts her too much. At church and in the group she has grown up with she is a giggly, gossipy student who would rather talk with her friends than cooperate with a teacher. A year ago she was baptized. Down underneath she loves the church although she is quick to complain about it and any youth activities she doesn't like. She likes the older boys—and younger ones, too, although those her own age seem juvenile to her.

By now at school she has a good sense of history and time span. She can put a number of facts together to form her own concepts when she puts her mind to it, although she doesn't concentrate well for very long periods of time. She has grown considerably more insecure in the last couple of years and seeks to conform to the styles, fads, and activities of her closest friends. She feels unhappy about some of her feelings of love-hate toward her parents. She also has guilt over some of her awakened sexual thoughts. She still relies pretty much on living by the authority her school and home put on her, but she is thinking for herself.

Jack

A sixteen-year-old junior in high school, Jack has been cut from the football and basketball squads in the past year. This has been part of a painful time for him. He has grown five inches during the year, and his coordination hasn't caught up with his larger body. Awkwardness shows up all over him even while several other boy friends his age are rapidly becoming more graceful and more agile. He has some acne that he hasn't been able to control. Put that together with his awkwardness and generally poor self-image and he has a hard time relating to the girls.

In fact, right now he is avoiding most contacts with them. If there is likely to be any pairing off at youth meetings, he doesn't go. If girls speak to him, he blushes and turns away. He is painfully shy. He rarely has anything to say in class, although his teacher has learned that he can come up with some surprisingly deep insights.

His parents have found that they can give Jack considerable freedom about when to come home at night, where he spends his time, and how soon he must get his homework done. They feel he is reliable in carrying out family responsibilities. At church he has so far avoided most serious discussions and actions that might lead him into a religious commitment. But he has developed some guidelines for living that show up clearly.

Linda

Meet Linda, who had to drop out of college just before her senior year and is now living with her widowed mother in her hometown and working as an assistant librarian. She is painfully aware that she is not the most beautiful girl in town. She has a lively personality and reasonably good features but is a bit overweight. On rare occasions she goes with her mother to church or to some social activity connected with the church. Otherwise she is having a most limited social life. She would like to marry someday and have a family, but right now the opportunities look limited.

The variety of situations among young adults her age is so wide that she finds few in this small town with whom she can be friends. Many of her old high school acquaintances have left town for school or work. Those who remain are preoccupied with new marriages or are following interests quite different from hers.

Deep inside Linda is somewhere on the borderline between being a law-and-order person committed to living by the rule book and developing her own ethics. She has not tested hers enough to know just how she might react in many situations. In fact, she is a bit uncertain about her self-image, who she is, and what she is becoming. She feels lonely and isolated. She is afraid that away from school and in this small town she is in some ways drying up, going to seed. She has thought about talking with someone besides her mother, whom she loves but despairs of, to see if she could find some help.

Marie

Marie is a middle-aged mother of three grown children and two grandchildren, all of whom live far away from the old family home where Marie resides with her husband. Marie's mother lives nearby but is in declining health and is a worry for Marie. Marie also worries about her husband, who is overweight and has high blood pressure and who doesn't, she feels, take very good care of himself. She herself is busy night and day, working at a dry-cleaning establishment, keeping house, and being active at church.

Marie has attended church most of her life and finds it her chief social outlet. She has taught young children at the church but is not teaching now because of her busy schedule. She does not read as much as she once did, filling her spare time in the evenings with television.

Back in school days she worked hard and made fairly good grades (she is a high school graduate), but she feels that she never has been a particularly deep thinker and that much of what is said at church and in her adult class is on some different wave length. She feels that she never is able to come up with good ideas of her own in class; she just doesn't have confidence in them. She tends to think in terms of people and events and objects more than ideas. She wants to know clearly what the Bible says for her to do or not do and has trouble when that is not clear.

Her health is not good these days. Her moods swing rapidly to wide extremes.

Ralph

After a long career as a high school teacher, Ralph retired last year. At about the same time his wife died. He has a daughter and grandchildren living nearby who have suggested he might want to move in with them now or at some time in the future, but he resists this idea. He wants to be independent of them although he does get lonely at times. He reads a lot, is actively interested in all the news, does some golfing and fishing in good weather. Sometimes he thinks about moving to a warmer climate but hates to leave his friends. He is bothered that his circle of close friends his age is diminishing. Some have died. Some have retired to other states. He is not making as many new friends as he once did, and it seems to him that since he is without his wife, he doesn't get involved in many social activities. It is a time of adjustment for him. He misses the school, the other teachers, the students, and the old daily routines.

Ralph is still a growing person in many ways. He is always picking up and dealing with new ideas. He is responsive in class. He has much to share, and he is respected for the contribution he has to make. He is pretty well aware of himself, both his strengths and his limitations. He has a well-developed, clear, personal philosophy of life of which he is totally convinced and by which he acts. He is aware of the limits on his strength; he works out regularly at the YMCA and tries to keep fit. He doesn't always eat well or regularly and hates to see a doctor either for checkups or for care when he is not feeling too well.

We Are Alike—and Different

What do the sketches of these eight persons suggest to us about who learners are, how they fit into our classes, and how we may most helpfully relate to them? We can take several different standpoints in sensitizing ourselves to our students (which is at the heart of what the teaching process is all about).

One such standpoint is viewing these persons as the highly unique and individualized creation of God, a foundational view that reaches into and interlocks with our other approaches to the individual student.

Another standpoint is to look at the lifelong persistent and rather permanent questions, issues, and characteristics that learners have.

A third viewpoint is to understand them as growing, developing, changing persons, following somewhat measurable but not universally binding patterns.

A fourth viewpoint involves us in seeing the individual within a larger social, historical, and current content of life involving both heredity and environment.

A significant fifth standpoint is to understand the transforming influences that may come into a life, often very quietly but sometimes with a sudden burst of energy or even trauma. Christian commitment and conversion sometimes seem to enter lives in this last way.

Let us turn first of all to the third of these approaches, the idea of personal development, which has been in the spotlight strongly in recent years. One developmental approach, in which Jean Piaget played a major early part, takes us down a cognitive or mental development track. Lawrence Kohlberg followed in that track to identify a moral development that is strongly cognitive.

Erik Erikson came at the developmental question from more of a psychological and sociological standpoint, dealing much with the emotional aspect in his description of eight ages of human beings.

Eventually these various approaches were brought together in an application to faith development, James Fowler being a major figure in this work. A wide range of developmental researchers have contributed in this field. Their work has been challenged by those who want to come at the individual's life pilgrimage in other ways. Nevertheless these approaches have been helpful in understanding growth qualities in individuals.

All these systems suggest that learners move along through growth at their own pace but with common characteristics. We can be ineffective and can even short-circuit the development process if we don't understand it and if we push or pull people along or assume they are ready for some things that they just aren't ready for yet.

The accompanying chart is a picture in very broad terms portraying realms of human development fairly typical of us all. It represents a rough flowing together of the thought of a number of persons who have been influential in describing ways we develop.[1] My purpose in writing this kind of volume is not to go into detail here, but simply to indicate how some understanding of human development can help us relate to persons in the classes we teach.

The chart Ways We Develop is intended to show a person moving out as he or she grows across a period of years from the self-centered base from which we all start to broader understandings and more mature ways of relating to the world around us.[2] It is not tightly related to particular age levels as it stands although there are common times in life when we tend to be in I and move to II.

Ways We Develop

I. The self as central.

Preoccupation with physiological needs, survival, security,
  safety.

Reflexive to prelogical thinking.

Acts out of self-interest: What's in it for me?

Obeys outside authority out of fear of punishment.

II. The self as belonging.

Legalistic. Obligation to obey external authority.

Gang stage.

Seeking to prove oneself; seeking esteem from others.

Concrete thinking.

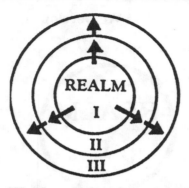

III. The self as independent.

Seeks to be independent of others, but has strong desire for social approval.

Development of self-esteem.

Self-assertion. Power/authority issues.

Abstract thinking.

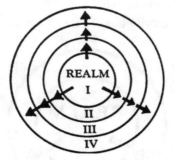

IV. The self as interdependent.

Has resolved or is resolving life issues in such directions as basic trust, industry, intimacy, and generativity.

Self-actualization.

Wisdom.

Living by inner principles and social contracts.

Serving and worshiping God out of love for him and others.

Obviously Realm I is a stage for persons in infancy and early childhood. Realm II is a common stage for children of elementary school years, but many normal adolescents and adults are also in it to some extent. Realm III is common for late adolescence and early adulthood. There is usually a crisis time, perhaps a real struggle, when we first burst through the boundaries from one realm to another. Some persons don't successfully make that leap at typical chronological ages and therefore may live out long years without moving past the barriers that would take them to a broader or more mature realm.

Some people are simultaneously living in more than one realm at a time in different aspects of their lives. In many ways we may return to our central base in the self in a momentary way or for longer periods of withdrawal. It does appear that once we have extended our horizons outward, such as in the realm of mere obedience to external authority as compared with living by inner principles, we tend to maintain ourselves at that higher level.

Christians will see a person's relationship to faith involved here. A life conversion may come as a person bursts from an inner realm to an outer one. We see a developing faith described in the Bible as whole peoples move from some of the primitive beliefs and practices in parts of the Old Testament to live increasingly by the Realm IV teachings of Jesus. While we are recognizing that teachers cannot pull persons from Realm I to Realm IV in their own strength, we may understand the power of the Holy Spirit to aid the person in that development.

In all of this we find useful implications for teaching. If second graders as a general rule are able to think only in concrete terms, it is not helpful to load them up with a lot of abstract ideas. If an adult gives all the indications of not being able to think in abstract terms, if that person is living by blind obedience to a code of laws primarily out of fear of punishment—then we need to deal with that person in those terms. We can't expect much fruitful exploration with such persons if we are erroneously assuming that they understand all about and are living by inner principles. That is a foreign world to them.

While a given class may all be in the same realm of development in general, the sensitive teacher would recognize the range of different realms in which members of the class are. The teacher would know that a general course can fit the common denominators in the class but that individual relationships are needed to relate to specific needs and concerns.

The chart doesn't present a goal for Christian education wherein we feel we must move all persons to some highly developed form of Realm IV. We will find adults with long experience in the church conscientiously leading lives based in any of the four realms described here. The developmental realms or stages are mainly useful in helping us to understand the learners we deal with and to recognize growth when it comes in response to the enabling, serving, modeling, and stage-setting we have done.

The eight persons listed here are living in different realms not always strictly according to age-level development. It would help us relate to them as teacher, friend, and guide if we could roughly identify them in appropriate realms.

Karen appears to be, appropriately enough, in the self-interest stage (Realm I on the chart). She will live by external authority out of fear of punishment and some desire to please. She certainly is not ready to live according to inner principles, although in an effort to please she might give that impression to some well-intentioned teacher who might try to help her live according to the law of love.

Though three years older than Karen, Randy may not be even as far along this path as Karen. His background and perhaps his inner schedule of maturation simply have not brought him along this far.

Mike, the fourth grader, appears to be deeply into the external authority, law-and-order area of Realm II. As such, the language of inner principles is probably not going to speak to him. He is at an appropriate place in his development and needs to be accepted at that place, just as all persons need to be accepted and understood for what they are even while we may envision greater things those persons can be and may some day become.

Sherry's disagreement with parents at thirteen may be an indicator that she is caught somewhere in law-and-order aspects between Realm II and Realm III and is resisting the outside authority. This may pave the way for a move on into the area where she can govern her life by inner principles or she may fall back, sometimes may even be crushed into obedience to a law-and-order system. She is moving into the abstract thinking age. She is working out many issues related to belonging, self-esteem, and esteem by others.

At sixteen Jack seems in some ways less mature socially than Sherry, who is three years younger than he. At the same time he has moved into a behavior pattern that seems in many ways self-directed (a Realm III concern). Yet he seems unable to enter into social contracts with others or with the church, feeling unwilling yet to give himself to it. Such is the freedom that we need to allow him, just as God has allowed it to him.

Linda reflects some of the increasingly wide variety that characterizes adults (with characteristics showing up from several realms in the chart). The longer we go through life, the more we move out of the prescribed limitations of childhood, the more varied life experiences we have accumulated, the more widely different persons we are likely to be. That hits us especially as we seek to plan and relate to young adults—some newly married, some with young families, some single but approaching marriage, some single with no plans in any other direction, some still in school, some in careers, some uprooted, some in old family situations. Linda has fears about whether she is going to stagnate now or move on into a generative life. She is at the same self-esteem point (Realm III) that many teenagers much younger than she are in.

Marie has a stagnation problem. An adult, her general lifestyle is caught in Realms II and III. Along with countless other adults in this television era her reading and other skills from school have actually declined. It also appears that she may never yet have reached the abstract-thinking point. She may not have gone beyond legalism in her moral reasoning development.

As Christian teachers we cannot relate to Marie in the same way we would relate to Ralph, whose abstract thinking, reasoning skills, and wisdom are more developed. In general Ralph has moved to a level of relative maturity in or near Realm IV. Not that life for him is without problems and constant readjustments. Far from it. He may be less flexible than he appears. He may have buried fears and worries deep inside himself. He may have unresolved developmental baggage he is carrying from his past. But in some ways he has "arrived," and teaching him needs to take his development into account.

Consider now the eight persons and the way they can relate to other students, how they are able to participate in class. It would be a mistake to assume that all of them can relate in the same way, to the same degree, with the same kinds of responses to teaching. Look back again and see if you can determine what kind of response you could reasonably expect from each person in a class where you are seeking to draw students out. Look again and see what kind of personal relationship with each learner might be most helpful. To whom do you need to give a little breathing room? To whom do you need to draw close? Whom do you encourage into new and experimental activities? With whom do you work to build up security? Again, the eight persons all have varying relations to Christ and the Christian community. Some may be seeing Jesus primarily as a rewarder of good and a punisher of wrong (Realm I). Some may be viewing him as the authority who tells us what is right and wrong (Realm II). Some may be understanding him as the person with whom we enter into a loving relationship out of which we decide freely and openly that we will follow him and his teachings in all that we do (Realms III and IV).

It makes a difference where people are. It also makes a difference just how much we think we can push, pull, nudge, or otherwise move them to new stages. We can help clarify, we can provide context, we can ask thought-provoking questions, we can forcefully proclaim God's word. But in the end it is the person who makes the choices and either moves on into the next realm or gets more or less permanently settled in the old one. When we are untimely in our remarks, when we awkwardly push and pull, we may in fact be putting roadblocks in the way of the development of the person.

Persistent Life Concerns

Now let's shift just a bit. For a while we've been noting individual differences along a common path of development. At the same time we all have much in common. We all face some questions and concerns that stick with us throughout life. We face some questions that we no sooner get wrapped up than they become issues again as new situations emerge.

Again we might check back through the eight learners who were sketched and note if we see some of these universal issues emerging as we read on or between the lines. Here are some questions that stick with us:

- Who am I? What makes up the real me? What's special about me? What's different about me? Am I really a child or an adult? How free am I? What does it mean for me to be a person?

- Do I really belong? Why do I so often feel like an outsider? What do I have in common with others?

- What is the meaning of my life? How can I find wholeness and purpose in it? How can I be free? I need to be independent but also interdependent—how?

- How does God relate to me, and how may I respond? What is the meaning of forgiveness? Who is God and how may I relate?

- What is my responsibility for the gospel and its spread? What is my responsibility toward people around me, toward the wide world?

- Where can I find dependable sources of truth?

- What is my final destiny?

- How can I tell right from wrong? How can I know the highest good for my life and others? What standards and values should I hold highest?

- How do I fit into this whole world around me—nature, authority, friends and family, church?

Such questions as these—and others—persist in just about everybody's lives, cropping up in different forms at different times and taking on fresh urgencies here and there. They form a basis of common concern that all teachers will be working on with all their students. Again you can trace these back through the eight personal sketches and find bits and pieces of them coming through, sometimes as a part of the developmental realm they are in, often as lifelong, persistent issues for everyone at every stage. We are dealing here with whole but growing and changing persons. For the sake of analysis we may put the microscope on the cognitive elements in their lives, but if we focus only on the intellectual capacities we do not have the full person in our sights. There are also the choice-making capacities, the emotional element in their lives, and even those nearly hidden intuitions and insights that are often the door for the spirit of God to work in our lives. In Luke 2:52 Jesus is described as growing in whole-person ways.

We are dealing with persons where the change may be slow, almost imperceptible, and where it may be sudden. It may be bubbling up from within, or it may be drastically affected by sudden onslaughts from outside. Great transformations may leap onto the stage of life in seemingly miraculous ways.

What Does This Mean for Teaching?

To sum up our observations of learners: Each one is an individual created by God worthy and different from all others. And yet learners do have some things in common. We all share some patterns of human development that we tend to follow in the midst of our individual differences. It helps for teachers to know about where the learners are in these realms for us to communicate effectively with them. All learners also have some common and persistent life concerns, needs, or issues.

Students share these, and that sharing allows for us to make group approaches that are relevant. Learners also have their own thing going in relation to God, Jesus Christ, the Holy Spirit, and the church. They are at various places in their response to God and commitment to God, but it helps if we are sensitive to where they really are. Their lives have been affected in relation to the transforming elements that have entered into their pilgrimage. Learners have their own skills, capacities, and readinesses for relating to others. Some move with confidence in groups; some are shy. Some are quite verbal; others cannot easily express themselves. Some are deeply involved without showing many outward signs.

We have been making some of the observations about what all

this says to teachers as we went along. Let us gather these together and perhaps face some new conclusions here.

1. We do not teach classes so much as individuals. It is important for us to know and relate personally with each learner, finding out where that person is on the pilgrimage of development, growth, Christian relationships, learning what that person's world is. It is important to spend time with each person and to become a real friend. At the same time our individual learners are in fact also in a group. Groups have climates and shared aspirations of which we need to be aware and for which we need to provide.

2. It is helpful to know and take into account some of the basic realms of human developmental. Identify where students are, where some may be stymied. This aids our communication and our understanding. At the same time we need to be careful not to lump learners easily into simple categories.

3. Knowing the learners, their common persistent life issues, and their diverse developmental patterns suggests that a variety of groupings and gradings may be helpful, that flexibility at this point is needed. Some intergenerational approaches that bridge between young and old are worthwhile and useful. Some rather closely graded approaches are good. In the church there is value in usually concentrating on peer group learning, somewhat broadly graded, usually involving learners of both sexes together (although there will be times when gatherings by girls only or by boys only may have short-term value).

4. If we understand that learners move from one realm of development to another largely through their own understanding and at their own initiative, then we know we cannot push, we cannot pressure very effectively in those directions. If we understand learning to be something learners must do for themselves, then we seek to set the stage for that. We cannot bring it about by ourselves. But we can invite. We can encourage. We can set the stage. We can pray.

5. If we know that there are some common patterns of development and some persistent issues, then we know enough to work at making the areas in which we teach relevant to as many students as possible.

6. If we believe that the learner is central in the process, then our

teaching places the learner in that spotlight rather than us as teachers. We can usually do our job better if we stay out of the spotlight. The classroom is not a place for us to perform to the applause of an audience. Instead, our work is to help the learners see themselves in relation to God. This means we provide ways for the students to speak out for themselves. We seek to set them exploring. We ask them leading questions: Why? How? When? We set up situations, provide experiences. We engage them in dialogue. We refer them to resources. We stand beside them. All of this, really, is teaching.

7. Given these understandings, we don't exert some rigid control in top-sergeant style. We start in with younger children to provide encouragement, exhortation, and correction. We may need to do some coaching and even provide some rewards and punishment.

But as time moves along, later in childhood, some of those earlier procedures have lost their value. Now we foster self-responsibility for each other and we model this with our own lives. To discipline, at its best, is to call people on through our own moral influence toward the utmost and highest for them. Finally, therefore, discipline is communicated to older children, youth, and adults who have made progress through dialogue and give-and-take.

Actually, woe to that class where the students line up rigidly and maintain a severe behavior, where we can hear a pin drop. Learning takes place better in a more relaxed atmosphere where all the sounds of human interaction by people exploring and discovering things are heard. Out of understanding response to the teacher and to each other, out of a desire to pursue learning, good discipline becomes a by-product. It develops within the students rather than being imposed from outside.

This does not mean that good and effective teachers and reasonably interested and involved classes will never face problems of class disruption, but an approach that seeks to attract students to learning will care for most ordinary discipline situations. When special discipline problems do arise, person-to-person dialogue is called for as we work out mutual solutions that get us past unwarranted disruptions of the learning process.

This kind of chapter is perhaps the most important one in any textbook on teaching. For the learner is central in the teaching process. The teacher is simply the helper, the facilitator, the questioner, and the resourcer.

TEACHING ON THE AGE LEVELS

You will note wide individual differences among the people you teach. You will want to avoid ending with just stereotypes in thinking specifically about them. The developmentalists have been most helpful to us in understanding learners, in helping us with clues about what the groups of children, youth, or adults we teach are like and how to relate effectively to them. Understanding growth, how people may be alike at different stages of their lives, considering how change may take place in their lives, being sensitive to individual differences, supporting and understanding the transformations and the conversions that can take place—these are all a part of the sensitive teacher's role.

Here are some insights about learners contributed by those who have studied them in recent years. They come from such divergent sources as Erik Erikson, Jean Piaget, Lawrence Kohlberg, Abraham Maslow, Brian Hall, James Fowler, James Loder, and John Westerhoff. And yet they have enough commonality about them to fit together in some description of the needs, concerns, and styles of learners at these ages.

Notes to Teachers of Young Children

The child begins life with a strong need to sense security and safety out of which comes a basic trust in others, starting usually with mother and moving out to family and friends and to God. This child moves on to a world in which the primal relationships of life are being worked out. Young children enjoy engaging in much play and fantasy. They are developing big muscle coordination.

From the beginning children are basically concerned with a world in which the self is at the center, but the horizons are being gradually pushed out. Actual experience is at the heart of things. The child learns not so much about Jesus and about religion as she or he learns to experience the love of Jesus and the kindness and care of the church.

Studying this chapter in the light of early childhood: Pick out

37

from this description of the early child one or two attributes of the young child that you and other children's workers can agree on. Edit the statement as you find necessary. For example, you might agree on a statement like this: "The young child needs to have a strong sense of security as a basis for venturing out into the world." Then write down or demonstrate the implications of that statement for the way you go about teaching. What can you do in your teaching and personal relationships with young children to undergird their basic trust, to feel that Jesus is there to help them, and to move with confidence among other children and in the church while away from parents?

Notes to Teachers of Elementary Children

Here is a general consensus about the development of the elementary child. What would you underline? question? adjust?

The elementary age child is rapidly developing basic competencies for going to school and for living. It is important for the child to achieve skills ranging from reading and writing to being able to do well in games and accomplish many tasks. Other people, in a widening circle beyond the family, become increasingly important to the child. Now the child seeks to please others widely, to get along, to achieve, to be well liked, and to belong and fit in with those around.

It is a natural time to join clubs, to affiliate, to sense a belonging to Christ and the Christian community. The world around can still be threatening, but the child may find satisfaction in solving some of the problems that the world seems to present.

Fantasy does not now play as large a part in the child's life as it did earlier. In fact during the elementary years, the child tends to be rather matter-of-fact and to be a concrete thinker. This undergirds the development of a strong sense of fairness and even a kind of legalistic approach to matters. While even the most intelligent children may seem to be able to talk about abstractions, they generally do not start to "think about thinking" and to engage in formal operations or genuinely abstract thought until they come toward the end of this period in their lives. They tend to live by rules or laws imposed from outside and also are likely to feel that good people should be rewarded and bad people punished in accordance with their deeds.

Studying this chapter in light of elementary childhood: Pick out one or more attributes of elementary childhood that you and other children's workers can agree upon, editing the statement as necessary. For example, you might say, "The elementary child has the strength of thinking concretely and matter of factly about religion." Then list or demonstrate some of the implications of that statement for teaching. In this case you might say, "Therefore, teaching will not burden this child with abstract or advanced theological concepts the child cannot really deal with." Or, "Concepts taught need to be demonstrated in practical, concrete ways."

Notes to Teachers of Youth

Here is a general consensus statement about the development of adolescents. What would you emphasize? question? adjust?

Youth years tend to be exciting times full of opportunities, but also troubling times for some teens and their families. There is a rapid movement shifting back and forth between childhood and adulthood. Actually this is an artificial time imposed by society, postponing the arrival of adult status for added education, job apprenticeship, and social maturation. With a growing sense of the need for independence the youth may come to increasing tension with parents, whether externally visible or internally held secret. This will not be obviously experienced at this time by all adolescents, however. It is a time of uncertain self-identity as young persons works on coming to terms with a changing body and a new relationship to the family and the rest of society. They want to give internal consent and to have increased voice in decisions affecting them. New mental powers make them able to handle formal thought operations, including abstract thought processes. The youth may begin to expand critical thinking and the ability to put together a combination of old ideas to form new concepts. Peers form a strong framework for whatever happens in the youth's life.

Studying this chapter in light of youth: Pick out from this description of youth one or two attributes that youth workers can agree on. Edit the statement as you find necessary. For example, you might frame a statement such as this: "Youth feel a need to achieve more independence and assume responsibility for their own actions." Then write down or demonstrate what implications these will have for teaching and personal relationships with the youth. One such in the example here might be this: "Give youth more voice in what is to be studied in class and how you go about it. Allow freedom to agree or disagree with certain issues that are raised in class without demanding agreement with the teacher."

Notes to Teachers of Adults

Here is a general consensus statement about the development of adults. With what would you agree most? What would you question? What would you adjust?

Developmentally, adults are a widely varied lot. No longer are they moving through the somewhat common patterns of school education with year-by-year requirements and common experiences. In most classes, even those labeled young-, middle-, or older-adult, the age range will vary widely. So will the experiences of the people—a wide range of jobs, marital and family patterns, health differences, and background.

Many young adults will be working out concerns with intimacy and unfinished developmental business from their younger years. They may be dealing with singleness or marital situations. Middle adults may be coming to new terms with the meaning of their mission in life and the spirit of generativity by which they are approaching things. Older adults may be seeing the wholeness in things, finding fulfillment in the directions they have been moving, in the growth of the seeds they have been planting all their lives. Others may be finding increased frustration in health and economic and spiritual issues.

In faith itself the adults may be moving through all the basic aspects of relating to faith—from the experiencing that began in early childhood, in the sense of affiliation that came with elementary school years, on into the searching of young adulthood and perhaps the sense of personal ownership that may then develop in adulthood. Somewhat predictable crises may emerge. The career and lifestyle with which one started the adult years may not seem to fit after a while. Somewhere in early midyears the question may arise, "Is this all there is really going to be to life? I better do something about it before it is too late." Basic satisfactions and wisdom may surface that the person seeks to share with others.

Studying this chapter in light of adulthood: Pick out from the description above one or two attributes that adult workers can agree on. Edit the statement as you find necessary. For example: "Adulthood is a time when people can make sure that the faith they now claim is really their own and not simply something they have adopted unexamined from parents or friends." Then work on implications of this for teaching adults. You might, for instance, make sure that adults have plenty of opportunities to form the theological values that they can fully own and allow those to guide their lives. Free discussion and valuing activities will support this. Being relevant and not just theoretical is important to adults, and classroom approaches should be checked out in the light of that requirement.

STUDYING THIS CHAPTER IN CLASS

Possible Goals
• To gain an increased understanding of who learners are, their individual characteristics, their common developmental patterns, their persistent life concerns.

• To gain skill in relating to learners.

• To understand how grouping and grading, discipline, and teacher-student relationships grow out of what we know about learners.

A Class plan
1. Look at several learners, their needs and concerns. (The eight learners described under "Look at Some Learners" may be portrayed through one of several means. You might ask class members to role-play those persons in an interview process. You might sim-

41

ply ask for eight reports on these people, their needs and concerns. To carry this out in a limited time schedule use only four or five cases from across the age span.)

2. Discuss the following: What common developmental patterns do these learners share? (Refer to the chart "Ways We Develop," and ask students to indicate which realms the eight learners appear to fall into. Note that the learners' development does follow an age-level chronology but not in a tight way. Some may remain in earlier realms for extended periods.)

3. Discuss the following: What differences emerge among these learners? (Still refer to "Look at Some Learners." List some of the differences shown by the group of eight on chalkboard or large sheets of paper.)

4. Discuss the following: In what ways are these learners related to Christ and the church? (Refer both to what the text says and how any role playing may have portrayed the Christian relationship. Tie this in with their development in other areas.)

5. Discuss the following: What stays the same for these learners throughout their lives? (See Persistent Life Concerns. Discuss how these common concerns may be served as the teacher relates to the person.)

6. List and discuss the implications of these learner qualities for teaching:

a. The importance of personal relationship between teacher and learner.

b. The value of a variety of grouping and grading, including intergenerational experience.

c. Understanding discipline as a dedicated style of learning growing out of good relationships.

d. Seeing the learner as central in the class, the teacher as a supporter.

Notes

1 Various social psychologists and educators have formulated systems that seek to identify and explain our common developmental characteristics and stages. Each is a little different or comes at the question from a somewhat different standpoint. If you are interested in pursuing these approaches in more detail, you might consult the following:

Motivation and Personality, Abraham Maslow

Childhood and Society, Erik H. Erikson

The Psychology of Intelligence, Jean Piaget

The Cognitive-Developmental Approach to Moral Education, Lawrence Kohlberg

The Development of Consciousness, Brian Hall

Stages of Faith, James J. Fowler

Moral Development Foundations, Donald M. Joy.

2 This chart was developed by Kenneth G. Prunty and the author, with a particular debt to Brian Hall, as a means of putting together some of the elements from various widely accepted developmental schemes. It is presented here as an elementary tool for teachers—use it in applying developmental concepts to your relationships with learners in your classes. The chart is not meant to be definitive or all-inclusive.

For everything that was written in the past was written to teach us,so that through endurance and the encouragement of the Scriptureswe might have hope.

—Romans 15:4

Chapter 3

Bridges to What We Teach

• Where shall I focus my teaching—on the Bible? on Christ? on persons?

• What do I want my students to learn most—facts? ideas? convictions?

• What teaching tools will best support my focus?

Relax. Shut your eyes. Let your mind wander for a minute. Now, if you're still awake, do a little dreaming about what teaching in an ideal situation might be. What would the place where you teach look like? What colors might dominate the room—if it is a room? What would the furnishings be? And, especially, what would you be teaching? Here we are thinking about courses of study, teaching materials, the content of our teaching. Here are some possibilities for you to think about:

1. Teach from curriculum materials supplied by the church.
2. Teach what the class wants to study—electives and the like.
3. Teach what the pastor recommends.

4. Teach whatever and however you feel led by the Spirit.

5. Teach what the Sunday school superintendent or the board of Christian education recommends.

6. Start with a prescribed curriculum but adapt it very freely to the situation.

7. Teach to meet perceived needs and readinesses of the students.

8. Teach the Bible.

9. Teach to meet life issues.

Perhaps you have a ready feeling about what you would actually do. Or perhaps you are still thinking about the choices and some possible combinations that might be made. Keep this matter in mind as we now make a visit to a church and a variety of approaches to content that are being used.

A Look at Some Classes

Let's take a walk through Seventh Street Church. It's Sunday morning and classes are in full swing. All around us are the busy, happy signs of people enjoying being together and finding satisfaction in shared learning experiences. Not that everything is calm and peaceful—watch out for those two boys headed this way. Laughing and scuffling, they almost knock us off our feet as they head for the door and out into the parking lot. But elsewhere we hear the laughter and earnest talk that says something good for Christian commitment and growth is going on here.

A. We look in the door at a class of first graders. Mr. Green is holding the Bible before him. He lays it, spine down, on a table and opens it carefully to the middle. As we stick our heads into the room, we hear him say, "And that's how you find the Book of Psalms in your Bible." He holds the book up and as the children gather around they spell out the word P-s-a-l-m-s.

B. Next door the kindergarten children, ages four and five, are in class. They have been playing in various interest centers. Over in one corner is a housekeeping center. In another corner is a simple jigsaw puzzle that several girls and boys have been putting together. In a window are some plants they have been caring for. But near the door one child has bumped into another. One cried and called the other one names. Now the two youngsters and the teacher are having a quiet conversation. They begin to smile at each other. Something about this incident; the lesson for the day, and the story that soon will be told, ties in with the scripture they repeat together: "Be kind to one another."

C. We round a corner and come to a class of young people. They are seventh and eighth graders. Two students stand in front of a large map of the Mediterranean world of Paul's day. They are tracing one of Paul's missionary journeys. Another student checks out their report by referring to her Bible. They are talking about events along the way. Two other students show simple stick figure drawings of those events.

D. Now we come to the church lounge where an adult class is meeting. Glancing through the door we see the teacher pointing to a poster that says in large letters *Hope*. As we listen we hear the class defining the word, comparing it with optimism and pessimism, and relating it to other terms. One man tells how he found new expectation in life when he learned what Christ could mean to him.

E. The class of fifth and sixth graders down the hall is looking at a chalkboard on which the Ten Commandments are written. They have been reading through the list, but each time more of the words have been erased. Now some of the commandments have been erased entirely, but together the class is still able to recite the whole list.

F. Next door, the third- and fourth-grade room has been set up as a learning center. The class members are studying the making of choices as followers of Jesus. Over in one corner a learning game calls for boys and girls there to make choices and see the consequences. In another corner students are listening to a recorded Bible story involving the choices that Jesus' disciples had to make in deciding to follow him. In another corner girls and boys are filling in a quiz with questions about this subject. In a fourth area, learners are working on posters about the importance of making good choices.

G. The older youth class appears to have just had a skit or a role play. The student "actors" are standing in the middle of the room. It seems that two of the students have just been delivering a basket of food to a needy family. Now the class is considering whether the persons delivering the food showed a good attitude in the process. Someone says, "I think they were too uppity the way they brought it in. They were looking down their noses at the poor people who had to have that food. I wouldn't like to receive a gift under those circumstances!"

H. Back to the upper elementary class. The group now seems involved in earnest conversation. Several students seem to be sharing. The teacher refers now and then to a Bible, now and then to a list of steps on the chalkboard. Finally they pray together. It is clear that they have come to a time of commitment.

Where Should Our Teaching Efforts Be Focused?

As you browse through these classes you see several different kinds of teaching going on. And several questions emerge about just how and what kind of focus you will have in your teaching. Some of these classes are engaged in direct study of the Bible. They are working with the book, gaining skill and ease in handling it, and finding things in it. They are involved with its teachings, interpreting them. Is this where the focus of our teaching should rest?

Other students are probing through the Bible, through hymn books, through the history of the church, and through direct doctrinal study to central matters of faith as these come to us from various sources. Their study is concerned with what we believe; all else radiates out from that. Is this where the focus of teaching should come?

Elsewhere the concern is with current life issues. The teacher is seeking to be right where the students are today. The focus is on the persistent life needs of students and dealing with those meaningfully. There is a heavy overlay of human understanding and development in such an approach. Is this where teaching-learning should focus in our classes?

48

Looking in on a class at any given moment, you might find any one of the approaches just mentioned taking place. Emphases vary. But if you stayed with the class for very long you might find the class moving through all of these. This happens with what is sometimes called a bridging or crossing-point approach. In it the effort is to bring the learners with all their needs and concerns into dynamic encounter with the living gospel so that they go away from that meeting changed by faith. The teacher cannot force this to happen but can carefully and deliberately set the stage for it to take place. This means our focus is on bridging between the student and the teachings of the gospel. So in course, unit, and session purposes we are looking to see if a crossing point is planned for. In the development of a session plan or in the way a learning center is set up to teach, we are checking to see if a bridge between life and gospel teaching has been built.

The implications of this for teaching are that we do plan to engage in meaningful Bible study, making sure that its meaning for life, its relevance, is strongly kept in mind. We do plan to place strong emphasis on the learners, who they are, what their needs and interests are, and what their development can be. But at the same time we are concerned that the gospel speak definitely to their lives. The flow of a session plan, the structure of a unit or course, therefore, can take any one of a variety of patterns to see that this is carried out. We shall get into this in some detail in chapter six.

Levels of Learning

Take another look at the series of classroom situations at the beginning of this chapter. Different kinds of learning are taking place at different levels. All are valid and essential parts of learning. In the church we want to check our teaching to see that we are not limiting our work or overbalancing our teaching on one level or another.

Fact Level (Information)

A basic and important but not exclusive area of learning is the fact level. At the heart of cognitive learning, this has to do with what we generally regard as factual knowledge. The teaching that one and one add up to two is a bit of fact-level or cognitive learning. Knowing the books of the Bible, the names of some of the great reformers in church history, memorizing John 3:16—these are fact-level learnings.

It is important that the Christian life be undergirded by factual content. Some church school curriculum systems concentrate in this area. Others sometimes go lightly here. To use an old cliché about classes and committees, we want to do more than sit around and pool our ignorance; we need fact-level content for our lives and our learning.

Concept Level

A second level of learning has to do with the development of concepts and ideas. Here the bits and pieces supplied to us in the form of facts are put together to shape ideas, outlooks, and perceptions that are in the area of personal understanding. If we put together various passages in the Bible with which we have become familiar to form some overall understanding about the meaning of God's love, we have built a concept. If we apply a set of facts to form a personal belief, if we paraphrase a Scripture passage into a personal affirmation about life, we have been working on the concept level. A balanced education includes both the factual and conceptual elements.

Living Level (Transformation)

A third level of learning has to do with the identification and development of personal convictions for living. This third form of learning is in the realm of students coming really to believe in and act on the facts and concepts they have gathered. Of course, valuable convictions may be formed apart from facts and concepts deliberately gathered. They may have entered the student's life in subtle ways through the environment and through the socialization process of living, interacting, and conversing with parents, neighbors, and peers.

In this process learners often decide to take a public stand for the concept under consideration, to commit themselves heartily to it, and to decide to act upon it out of conviction and not merely out of duty. In such an approach learners often are asked to set priorities among various good alternatives, to stand up for them, to try to convince others about them.

Clarification of the values we already have is important. Often we have within us the seeds of belief and practice that could be meaningful guidelines for our lives, but we haven't clearly identified them and put them to work. It is worthwhile for us to know those values that are important to us, to bring them out into the open, and to live by them.

Learning, as fostered in the church, is going to be concerned to move beyond values clarification to the formation and development of worthy convictions. We are going to be interested in bringing learners face to face with those basic virtues for which the Christian community stands, the affirmations we have reached, the styles of life that people have assumed in light of the gospel. And out of this, learners may choose to make some changes in the direction of those affirmations, those community commitments that they find important. In this sense they go on building up their own values as long as they are learning, growing persons.

Put It All Together

This also means that the content of what the learners will be considering, the stuff of Christian teaching, needs to be draw from all three levels of learning. Included will be the foundation blocks of information that come at the fact level. Here will be the walls and windows of insight that come at the concept level. Over all will be the roof of transformed living that caps it all off. These three aspects of learning will be cemented together into structures of usefulness and meaning for the learners, something they have put together for themselves. Those structures will be used actually for living out their lives.

Very often, therefore, the material that is to be studied will be most helpful if it comes to the learner with considerable attention to the life meaning it communicates. Likewise, much use of the experiences of persons is important. Illustrations from life, dealing with life problems, and the application of basic principles to specif-

51

ic situations—these are all important in fostering effective learning and in determining the content of teaching in the church.

Ultimately the concepts we learn move out of the columns of statistics and off the printed page to take on personal meaning. They finally involve us in living out what we know.

We've a Story to Tell

Not many teachers are professional jugglers. We may not be able to keep three objects bouncing gracefully in the air at the same time. So we may focus only on the facts. Or we may deal only on concepts. Or we may seek transformations without a basis in real knowledge. One of the most profound and telling ways of coming at the important three levels of learning and of approaching the learner as a whole person is through stories.

The heart of the content of our teaching is the story of Christ, the gospel. It all grows out of the long story of God's people and the stories of their lives and the events they have passed through. These are not meant to be merely illustrative but to be at the central core of what we teach.

What we intend to teach at its heart is the biblical story as it comes in contact with the whole person who is the learner. That suggests the bridge-building content of what we teach—the meanings, the values, and the data of faith all linked together.

Note the biblical heart of this. Written across the centuries, the Bible came out of a culture that was story-oriented. Picture the ancient Hebrew families sitting around their campfire at night while the patriarch recounted the great events and reminded his hearers of the significant people in their heritage. Here in many chapters was the story of how God dealt with his people. While the Old Testament includes the laws and practices of the Hebrews and while it includes the wisdom of the sages and the proclamations of the prophets, all is set in the context of the story of God's people. The focus in the Bible, and therefore in the content of our teaching, is largely on the relationships as portrayed in events and personalities between God and his people and among those people. The Bible, then, is more a book of relationships than of precepts. That has far-reaching implications for how we teach. We teach more by working with relationships than by recitation of facts or concepts.

The New Testament continues in this narrative fashion. At the center of the Bible for Christians stands the gospel, the good news of Jesus Christ, his coming to earth, his ministry, teachings, miracles, dealings with people, his death and resurrection. That is story, the gospel story, the truth communicated through time and relationships. These are stories more significant than mere factual reports. Then comes the story of the spread of the early church and the reflection of the letter writers upon that origin and its spread. Everywhere we find story, metaphor, and symbol.

This is no accident because the story approach, the emphasis on event and person and the broad human feelings engendered, is a natural and major way to appeal to our whole selves. Direct appeals to action and exhortations to make right choices may appeal to our need to choose and act. Yet other large areas of our personalities—our feelings and our intellect—are left untouched. A more whole approach, such as the story style, can involve the person in all her or his feelings, intuitions, perceptions, intellectual conclusions, and commitments. The story approach operates in a unified way on all those levels.

This is not to ask that teachers turn simply into illustrators and sharpen their skills to be entertaining storytellers. Rather, it is to invite the teacher to a growing awareness of the great story of the faith that she or he has to share and to sharpen skills and awareness in the narrative process. Concerned teachers will find varied media by which to tell the stories—dramatics, reading, role playing, audiovisuals, and the like. The teacher will not allow the students to sit back as passive hearers of the story only but to be active participators in it. Learners increasingly will be able to reflect on their own stories and to identify with the great and small stories of the faith.

This is at heart a biblical approach. It is also a theological undertaking. It is God-focused in reviewing the story of how the Lord has dealt with his people. Systems of theology may reflect in logical ways upon the story and seek to interpret it philosophically, but the story is the original basis for it all.

The teacher looks at a basic story approach and asks the practical questions. Even though the story idea brings to us an understanding of God's mighty acts in history and his personal relationships with people, what is there about the story approach that makes it central for my particular work?

Think, for example, about a parable of Jesus and what it does to appeal to us as learners:

1. Stories usually have touches of the common everyday life, little things that take us back to our early memories, our common experiences of everyday life, the way we tie in with our culture.

2. Stories touch us in all parts of our being. They give us something to think about. They give us something to feel. They probe into our innermost being and arouse our sense of intuition about what is real for us in a situation.

3. Most of us really love a story, certainly a funny one, even a sad one. Stories are interesting. They arouse our curiosity. They attract us. Look at the ratio of stories on commercial television compared with other types of shows. And most of the other programs provide a narrative approach and are about people and their doings.

4. Stories bear repeating. It is far easier for most of us to recall a story and pass it along than to remember the steps of someone's logical argument. We remember stories. They stay with us. They may even gain value across the years.

5. With their universal themes and approaches, stories remind us that we all share much in common. Young and old can join in understanding and enjoying a story, each person on her or his own level. Persons can learn of differing cultures and viewpoints with greater understanding through our great stories, with their common ingredients and common appeal.

6. We can identify with stories. We tend to put ourselves into them. We may live and breathe, struggle and weep and laugh with the hero or some other person in the story with whom we identify. God can come closer to us as both teachers and learners through stories.

7. Stories provide perspective. They can lead us out of ourselves and then help us look back at the situation from which we have come. Through identification we first find ourselves in a story, but by seeing it progress we can stand off and see origins from the past and possible outcomes in the future. We get a larger picture.

In short the story idea is a strong basis for ministry through teaching. God is revealed and his people come alive as revealed in their encounters with each other. All this takes place in their conversations, reactions, and participation in events of great magnitude or small bits of life. The teacher may be much helped by seeing that the content of what is to be taught is at heart story—truth communicated through events, feelings, persons, and relationships. These are stories to be read, told, acted out, reflected on, retold, interpreted, and enjoyed. They are central in the teaching-learning process.

A Plan for Content

Flow, Balance, Comprehensiveness

When we plan meals or set up a diet, we are concerned to have some variety in what we eat. We want a balanced diet. We want to be sure we include all the essential vitamins, minerals, and other food elements. Much the same is true of what we undertake in church. Recalling again the types of teaching we saw in the classrooms visited at the beginning of this chapter, we did observe a variety of approaches and subject matter. We could not discern broader patterns, other than that it was unlikely that these classes were all studying exactly the same subject matter on the same Sunday.

Naturally we are concerned that learners benefit from whatever wise planning we can give them. We need to bring them appropriate subject matter relating to where they are in life and their ability to learn and use it. We want them to cover all the areas of Christian learning we deem important for them to have experienced. We want enough variety so that their attention is kept and their appetite to keep on learning is whetted. At the same time, we don't want such a rigid system that the emerging needs, the momentary and passing interests of students, are neglected.

It is good to give attention to a carefully planned and wise pattern for flow, balance, and comprehensiveness in church teaching and learning. At the same time we need to leave room for flexibility and spontaneity as teachers and students relate to one another.

Uniform? Independent? Coordinated?

In planning for Christian learning across the church, we can take three basic routes with a curriculum plan. First, we could set up a uniform plan by which everybody studies just about the same thing on the same Sunday morning.

That was the dream and the ideal when the International Uniform Lesson system was established in the last century. It has some advantages. Teachers can be helped directly through lesson annuals and other aids and through teacher meetings across age levels to prepare their lessons. Pastors and other administrators can readily know exactly what is being taught, and they can plan supplemental activities, even sermons, accordingly. Learners who move or visit elsewhere in churches using the same system can proceed with their learning flow on an uninterrupted basis. Family discussions and worship activities can readily pick up on these common teachings. Occasional intergenerational activities can be held and stay right in the stream of what is being studied everywhere. The unity of the Sunday school and the church can be built up.

A uniform system across the Sunday school has disadvantages as well. It fosters a certain rigidity that cannot easily bend to meet individual needs or class wide concerns as they emerge. It means that kindergarten children and adults must be studying just about the same thing despite the overwhelming differences in interests, concerns, and abilities.

We have certain times of greatest need and greatest readiness for certain learning; a uniform system rigidly followed has difficulty serving such needs.

A second approach to planning across the church for Christian learning would allow each class or at least each department to go its own way. This can take a variety of forms. It may simply mean that each class or each teacher or the local Christian education board or committee decides what it wants to study on an age level. Youth and adult classes might follow an elective course approach. They choose books or courses that seem to meet the needs they feel at the moment.

Down through the younger age levels, teachers or others might select curriculum materials that happen to fit their own teaching styles, what they feel to be the needs and interests of their students. This approach has the advantage of allowing learners themselves or those fairly close to the learners to choose what they would be most interested in and concerned about. It has an advantage of flexibility. It can move fast to cover emerging needs. It allows a degree of freedom to choose what people most want to study.

The freewheeling, independent approach has certain obvious disadvantages. Learners, teachers, and others who might make spur-of-the-moment choices often don't have the big picture in focus. They don't see how what they teach this Sunday and this year may need to fit into a long learning track that the learner follows for a number of years. They may miss out on a plan that would cover a broad spectrum of biblical teaching, provide a balanced educational diet, and move systematically through a set of materials carefully planned to meet learners' needs as they go through various developmental stages.

Following the independent approach, learners may choose materials that deal with surface issues of concern to them right now and never get to the deeper issues and needs that are important for their overall development. A comprehensive program is lacking. Administratively and for the Sunday school order secretary, it becomes a curriculum chaos. There is little sense of unity, of learning community fostered by this approach. Great gaps in one's learning can emerge, but hardly ever are these recognized until it is too late. Overlappings can occur, duplicating efforts as a learner moves from one class or department to another.

A third approach seeks some of the best elements of both the uniform and independent approaches. It calls for the local church's curriculum process to be focused around a central, carefully worked out curriculum plan. All the courses of study are planned to relate to each other, to provide tracks for learners to follow, with good attention to comprehensiveness, sequence, and balance. At the same time each class isn't forced into a rigid mold of having to study exactly the same thing on Sunday morning whether that is appropriate for the age level or not. A central objective such as the one described in Chapter 6 ties the curriculum plan together.

In this third approach learning tracks are carefully worked out to bring learners in a balanced way through all the areas of the Bible appropriate for their learning, through great concerns of the church and life issues. By using a bridge-building approach where the concerns of the gospel are constantly brought to the needs of the students in an open-ended way, relevancy with students is maintained. By using some common emphases in quarters across the year and by relating courses directly to age levels but with an eye to where the individual students are, the learners, their families, and the church can benefit from having learners studying together in a common area.

Classes are most effective when they are not bound by a rigid theme, a tight and inflexible focus on a common subject, but when they are linked by a common way of looking at curriculum. That means a shared objective, some common themes, and even an occasional week when all are studying an intergenerational topic. This is a coordinated approach.

Any such program also has its own disadvantages. Classes and teachers don't have freedom to study entirely what they want. While there is open-endedness toward student interests and concerns, the class can't go totally in that direction; it persists with basic courses. The administrative advantage of having detailed similarity across age levels doesn't apply fully here.

In every approach to teaching/learning and its content we are forced to choose which advantages and disadvantages we want to deal with. As may be obvious to you by now my preference is for a coordinated curriculum approach, rather than either the totally independent or the totally uniform patterns. A coordinated curriculum approach offers reasonable flexibility and strong emphasis on meeting developmental needs and individual differences, while at the same time providing some sense of good sequence, balance, and comprehensiveness.

TEACHING ON THE AGE LEVELS

Notes to Teachers of Young Children

Here are two sample approaches to the teaching of content to young children.

Plan and Reflection. Play is an extremely important element in the learning process. It is the basic content of a child's learning. Play is the world of children. Play is their basic way of learning. (Perhaps this element could even be helpfully stronger in some adults' lives.) Add to this study moments in reflection on what has happened in play and what it has taught and we really have a basic approach to content for the young child. In play the child is practicing sharing, relating to others, carrying out projects, practicing being other people and fulfilling roles in the world. Content for the young child is in fact experience.

Story Hearing and Story Doing. The story circle provides a basic approach that can reach the whole of the young child. Stories about people can lead to identification. Stories about Jesus can help the young child experience him and his ways. Acting out stories or parts of them adds meaning and helpful involvement.

Studying this chapter in light of early childhood: Using others in your study group to role play, demonstrate an early childhood teaching situation of about five to ten minutes' duration. Then together reflect on what happened, particularly concerning the actual content of teaching. Consider how method and content flow together in an almost inseparable way in this kind of approach to young children. Consider also what levels of content are involved here—facts, concepts, or transformation. Consider what part the crossing point or bridge-building idea played.

Notes to Teachers of Elementary Children

Here are two sample content approaches to elementary children.

1. Reading, Hearing, Repeating Stories. This combination of approaches to the elementary child does several things. It allows the child to use developing skills such as reading. The child can also be given a chance to write a story or complete a story someone else has started, using other developing skills. The child can use

listening skills to hear a story and then to repeat back or otherwise demonstrate those listening skills. This ties in with the child's desire to achieve competency and his or her focus on the concrete rather than the abstract elements in learning.

2. Role Playing. Most elementary children enjoy drama and role play activities, especially now more than in the increasingly self-conscious years ahead of them in early adolescence. They can put themselves in someone else's shoes and find specific ways of demonstrating those views through role play. The elementary child's growing sense of fair play can come into this picture. Children can come to feel deeply what otherwise might seem to be merely theoretical matter.

Studying this chapter in light of elementary childhood: Pick a topic and plan a five- to ten-minute demonstration of a teaching procedure with other members of your study group role playing the parts of elementary children. Consider whether your method was on the fact, concept, or transformation level. Evaluate how the bridging between the content of the gospel and life practice may have worked out.

Notes to Teachers of Youth

Here are two sample content approaches to adolescents:

1. The Forum or Panel Discussion. In this approach various class members prepare in advance and present varying aspects of or views on an issue. They may involve peers in small groups in preparation of their presentations. A large class may form small groups to discuss the issues raised. Youth's growing ability to deal with abstract concepts and their increasing desire to search out aspects of their faith for themselves feed into this activity. In the process content is brought through research and pooling of information in the forum or panel. Varying viewpoints may be dealt with and perhaps reconciled or used as a spur to further research and discussion.

2. The Case Study. Perhaps a problem situation is presented in narrative form. The youth learners become involved with it as they live through the situation, weigh the problems involved in it, search for a range of solutions, and seek to apply those. The content

involves the original story and the resources provided for them to turn to as possible solutions. They use their growing life experiences and their abstract and critical thinking processes in making choices in connection with the case study.

Studying this chapter in light of youth: Pick a topic and plan a five- to ten-minute demonstration of a teaching procedure with other members of your group role playing the parts of youth. Then consider what level the procedure was on—fact, concept, or transformation. Consider what part bridging between life and content of the gospel played.

Notes to Teachers of Adults

Sample content approaches to adults:

1. The Mini-lecture and Discussion. This procedure has the potential of bringing into the class needed information as a basis for discussion but staying within the rather short attention span most of us have for lecture material. The lecture can be illustrated by slides, charts, or posters. It might last about five minutes. Then one or a brief series of very carefully worded discussion questions can be offered (in large classes small groups could undertake to answer these questions and get wider involvement). The questions themselves ought to be manageable by the group in the time allowed and be genuinely open to varying answers as arrived at freely by the discussing group. The information presented in the lecture ought to provide data useful in dealing with the question but not dictating the final conclusions that the class might reach in discussion.

2. Brainstorming-Toward-New-View Development. One of the most basic approaches to foster creativity and to gain wide, supportive participation is the brainstorming approach. It can be used to bring in content to a discussion from the wide variety of experiences and background knowledge already possessed by adult class members.

Here we choose a topic with many possible facets as we seek to bring those together in fresh combinations. You could brainstorm new ways, for instance, by which your congregation could reach out to needy people in the community. Invite learners to respond out of their own backgrounds and contacts. Most adult classes would have a rich variety here.

Studying this chapter in light of adulthood: Pick a topic and plan a five- to ten-minute demonstration of a teaching procedure with other members of your study group role-playing the parts of adults of different ages. Then consider how the various levels of content in learning would have played a part—fact, concept, or transformation. Explore also how bridge-building between life issues and the content of the gospel would be related in the approach.

STUDYING THIS CHAPTER IN CLASS

Possible Goals
- To see where the focus may come in the kind of content we deal with in teaching.

- To survey the variety of content and approaches to teaching it that are carried out in the church.

- To survey different levels of learning and the kind of learning content that goes with these levels.

- To examine what relationship should exist between courses across age levels—uniformity? independence? coordination?

A Class Plan
1. Ask small groups (two or three persons) to select something to teach to the rest of the class as a demonstration. (The groups will pick up a fact, concept, or value to teach to the rest of the class and designate the rest of the class for what age level they are to pretend to be. They will select a method for teaching it and then carry it out. For ideas on what to do, class members could refer to the teaching situations described following A Look at Some Classes (p. 46ff). An alternate approach is simply to study the classes described in the text.)

2. Check out the demonstrations for where they were focused—on the Bible, on the students, on bridge-building, elsewhere? (Use guidelines from the section Where Should Our Teaching Efforts Be Focused? in the classroom samples in the text. The following would be the focus: A, Bible; B, person or life-centered now, moving toward a crossing point; C, Bible; D, crossing points or bridge-building; E, Bible; F, mixed; G, person or life; H, crossing point or bridge-building.)

3. Discuss what levels of learning each demonstration was on—fact? concept? transformation? (See the section Levels of Learning for guidance here. In the cases suggested in the text, the following are the levels used: A, fact; B, concept, possibly transformation; C, fact; D, concept; E, fact; F, a mixture; G, concept; H, transformation.)

4. Decide what kind of curriculum plan the demonstrations reflect—uniform, independent, coordinated. (See the discussion under the section Uniform? Independent? Coordinated? Looking at the classroom samples across the age levels, it is obvious that they are not on a uniform system. We cannot tell whether they are in some planned and coordinated relationship or reflect each class going its own way. You can discuss the advantages and disadvantages in each system.)

5. Ask students to give priorities to other principles involved in choosing content for study. (Note further discussion under Flow, Balance, Comprehensiveness. How important do the students see these as being? What contribution to good learning can be provided when courses are organized with these qualities in mind? What is the priority of narrative in our content? What is the most appropriate use of the Bible—as a starting place? as an answer? as a source for life relationships?)

Make me to know thy ways, O LORD;
    teach me thy paths.
Lead me in thy truth, and teach me,
    for thou art the God of my salvation;
for thee I wait all the day long.
                              —Psalm 25:4–5

Chapter 4

Bridges to Ways We Learn

• *Why do some smart people seem to learn more, and more easily, than others?*

• *How can I help people to learn?*

• *Why do some people like to do active learning and others hate it?*

What have you learned lately? We do keep on learning things—at twenty, fifty, seventy. And where and how have we been doing this learning? For most of us this may have come through practical experience. But we also learn from books, newspapers, and even TV. It is to be hoped we have even learned something new about our faith in recent days. There is a mystery about learning that has never been fully opened up. But we are always learning more about learning. And that affects the way we try to teach in the church.

A teacher can help the process of genuine learning in many important ways. We can provide students with information. We can seek to stimulate their interest. We can reward desirable learning behavior and punish poor learning practice. We can set the pace in learning as a part of a community of study. We can do what is commonly known as teaching, which involves all these things. But students have to do the actual learning for themselves.

This has clear implications for how we teach. If we believe that we can automatically cause learning to take place simply by presenting information, then we will do a lot of that. If we believe that we can cause learning by presenting facts and stimulating the learners by rewards for their going through learning motions and punishments when they do not, then we will do much of that. If we believe that learning is a project the learners must undertake for themselves because they really want to, then we will simply try to do the very best teaching job we can and rely on the learners to carry out that learning task for themselves.

This means that we do our best to provide content for the learner to use in the most effective way possible. It means we work at encouraging them to learn. It means that we spend much time and energy trying to understand how students go about learning and fitting our work in with that process. Learning is a complex undertaking. Different learners apparently learn with varying efficiency depending on the methods involved and the kind of things they are seeking to learn.

At the very heart of what we as teachers and agents for the spread of the Kingdom through education do is to encourage learning. We are considering learning here to mean changes, initiated by the learner, more or less permanent, and in a direction that the learner values. It can involve a change in information, in concepts, in attitudes, in behavior, in commitments—all that is important in the whole person.

We tend to take on teaching assignments in the church that place us in charge of groups. Learning from peers and with the stimulus of groups around us is an important aspect of most people's learning, but the process remains a highly individual and personal matter. As teachers we do not have automatic passes into the hearts and minds of our students with prescriptions for change. The learner controls that gate and admits what comes knocking only as that person chooses to do so. It would be dishonest and in the long run ineffective to try to slip learning through that gate through trickery and dishonest manipulation.

We hope that the learner will be open toward what we have to teach. We can encourage openness and the sense of trust that is called for by ourselves being open, by being honest and trustworthy in our teaching relationship. The teaching climate we build can contribute to that.

Nor is learning merely a mental process. It involves the whole person. Certain objectives may cover specific information to be memorized, tasks to be accomplished, concepts to be evaluated. But in general we are seeking for the whole person to learn. Hence we teach not just for intellectual insights, but we also seek to take into account the feelings, the insights, the commitments of the learner. In order to support that person as a learner, to facilitate the learning process, we seek to see that person as a whole. We seek to see that person realistically as he or she now is and as that person has potential for growth. We want to build persons up, help them grow in self-esteem. At the same time we help them commit to a discipline that lends muscle and purpose to their learning process.

Learning Tasks

One basic way of understanding the learning process is to see it as a group of tasks a learner undertakes in the process of change. The tasks a person may undertake in order to learn have sometimes been listed in five categories. Learners may engage in any one of these without reference to the others and in any sequence. Nevertheless a sequence is often involved here as the learner moves through learning tasks two through five in a few moments' time, across one class session, or across a longer course of study.

Learning by Listening and Responding

A general, umbrella kind of learning task is to "listening with growing alertness to the gospel and responding in faith and love." Interpreted in a broad sense, this is what we are always doing when we seek to learn within the context of Christian education. This is not usually a passive soaking up of data. It is really hearing from all the things that speak to us out of our environment, out of the media to which we expose ourselves. That hearing involves thinking over critically what we hear. It means weighing it against all the other data that has come. It involves engaging in some dialogue with the sources of information.

Teachers can foster the listening habit by seeking to provide a setting in which it is easy to listen. They try to make concentration possible, not by an ironclad discipline of classroom silence, but through an atmosphere in which it is easy for ideas to be heard. This means that teachers cause learners to want to listen. This can't be done by tricks or maneuvers but is encouraged by direct stimulation and interest. Teachers will spend much effort seeking to help the learner develop listening skills. The learner comes to ask what the communication is really saying. What is being left unsaid? What is being said between the lines? Why was this particular word used? What are the important ideas here? What are less important? Is this the truth? How is this a part of a larger picture?

The other part of that umbrella learning task speaks about responding in faith and love. It is not enough to listen actively; the listener is asked to make a response, to act or speak in some life-changing way. In the Christian setting that response will be characterized by a high relationship of faith in God and love for God and all those around us.

There are those who say that listening hasn't really taken place until the persons receiving the original communication have registered it in their minds and have provided some feedback to the sender. All of this is to say that communication is a basic process in learning. Communication is a two-way street. Communication methods that facilitate feedback are therefore usually the most effective.

Learning by Exploring

Coming under the umbrella learning task of listening and responding to the gospel with alertness is a series of additional learning tasks that spells out the process in more detail. One of these involves exploring. It is appropriate to explore widely in light of the gospel. The teacher's work here is to open the avenues for wide exploring, to suggest alternate paths that can be followed, to inspire and offer challenges for the way of exploring.

Typical activities here would include doing some research in the Bible and elsewhere through a process in which final answers are not automatically provided. Experiments fall in this area. Taking surveys, interviewing people about their opinions, going on field trips are all forms of exploring.

Learning by Discovery

This involves finding some new insights. While the spirit of exploration, seeking, and openness to new insights is to be fostered, that learning task does not stand entirely on its own. It moves on to making some findings, to arriving at some meanings and values, to reaching some secure destination. This does not stand apart from exploring, either. We don't have the luxury of simply encouraging learners to go out and find for themselves something that we have predetermined they should find. We run the risks that they will discover things that are different from what we intended or at variance from what our own discoveries have been. But we do want them to move beyond seeking to finding, and in the realm of Christian education we want that to be true, meaningful, and worthwhile for their lives.

Discovery activities might involve students with in-depth study of the Bible, in paraphrasing a Bible passage while checking study aids to make sure they are staying within the realm of its basic meaning. It means goal-setting activities and checking out how we are doing in moving toward goals. It means using resource materials and putting together concepts growing out of resources we have provided.

Learning by Becoming Convinced

We don't fully learn just by exploring and discovering and finding something out there somewhere. What is learned is to take on meaning personally for us and become a part of our own lives. Here valuing kinds of learning methods come into play. Activities that help us move beliefs from a merely intellectual level into convictions we really feel are needed at this point. So the valuing activity asks the students individually to take a stand for what they believe. This happens through putting ourselves publicly on the line for something.

Whatever the approach, the effort is for the learner to get past just knowing what someone else believes, beyond just knowing the facts and the concepts, to the place where it can be said, "This is what I stand for with all my strength!"

Learning by Acting on Convictions

The ultimate learning is when a person decides to act on convictions. We are going to do something about what we have learned. We are going to accept responsibility for some things happening both on the social and the personal levels. We expose these to the light of the gospel. Learning activities that relate here are classroom commitment times, various acts of worship that can take place in the session, service projects by the class, and individual actions putting into practice insights gained from the session.

This is a difficult learning task to see fully carried out. We tend to stay theoretical and intellectual in class more often than we put shoes on our learning. Or, teachers may stand back hopefully and figure that it is somebody else's responsibility to see that people in their classes get involved in actual Christian practice somewhere else. That may often need to be the case, but there should be a strong bridge between the class and practical Christian living. Only in this way may we know that learning has fully taken place.

In Support of Learning

While teachers cannot do people's learning for them, there are some things about the learning process the teacher can take advantage of in order to encourage learning at its best. The wisdom of the human race about this process has, after all, been accumulating for centuries. Go back once again to the survey of eight Sunday school classes near the beginning of the preceding chapter and see what kind of supports to the learning process are being used. We will get into a discussion of specific learning activities and an evaluation of them in the next chapter, but here we are looking at time-honored skills and insights that undergird learning. Which of the following list do you find taking place in the classroom situations described? We shall discuss some of these briefly as means of bringing to bear these approaches on your calling to teach.

Take Advantage of Readiness. "Strike while the iron is hot" says the old proverb. Teach at the opportune moments. Teach when the students are ready. Teach about immortality just at the time when one of your learners' grandmother has died. All kinds of readinesses of that sort arise in the lives of your class members, and you can take advantage of those as you become thoroughly acquainted with them and their lives. Or teach about the role of Israel in the world just as girls and boys develop their first strong sense of history and the sweep of geography and how those mingle. A likely early readiness time for that might come in fifth grade. It might be difficult to teach meaningfully about that in the third grade. At the same time we know there are individual differences, that each learner is on a personal line of development. It pays to be aware of the process and to relate to it. A learning principle here is to start at likely times of peak interest. This means staying alert to the students and their concerns. The right moment! It means not following the curriculum plan slavishly but using it to full advantage to bridge to the needs of students as you perceive them.

Try to Be Relevant. This bit of guidance grows out of the readiness issue just discussed and like it calls us to be closely attuned to the needs and interests of the learners. What is of most importance and most interest to the learners in your class right now? Tie in with that. Perhaps you will start your teaching with that and then move to related and basic insights from the Christian faith. Teachers of youth and adults have found this to be of special importance in some contrast to students in elementary classes who have been conditioned to deal with whatever comes up in their daily classes at school. Adults want to feel that, somehow, what is being considered here in this class setting has some real meaning for their lives. It can't just be left to be theoretic, important as that may be overall.

Ask for Learning by Doing. As our basic definition of learning implies, we need to be personally active in the learning process. Most of us learn better by doing than by just reading or watching. Whenever we have an opportunity to encourage a learner to do something in connection with the concept under study, we will be helping that person. This should be more than busywork. Practice applies particularly to skills. Remember that skills can run a range from sewing to finding verses in the Bible to showing kindness to a child in dirty clothing. Doing can also involve experiencing. Learning at its richest and fullest involves living out the concepts involved, being a part of the story. And this ranges from the small child to the older adult.

Encourage Learning by Reflection. Important as doing is, the learning process is not complete with simple activity. The doing part works best when it is tied in with reflection on the action, on thoughtful planning for further action. There is a rhythm that goes back and forth here. We need to give students time for the significance of what they've been doing to sink in. It is perhaps typical North American style to hurry our students along too much. It may take some time for all the parts of the puzzle to fall in place. Times for quiet reflection may accomplish wonders. The passing of a little time from one session where heated discussion took place until the issue comes up again is helpful for the learning process.

Expect Learning through Socializing. Much more than half of what you and I have learned in our lives has come from outside the school and church classroom. It has come from talking with our friends, relating to other people, somehow imitating those we admire. The ordinary give-and-take of daily life is the school in which we learn most of life's basic lessons and special skills. This means that families do a lot of teaching. So do friends at school and work. It also means—and this is particularly significant for those called to teach in the church—that considerable learning goes on in the odd little moments of friendly conversation around the class and even at class parties. Those unplanned moments that are scattered across the Sunday school period and that come at its beginning and end should be counted as a part of the curriculum.

Involve All the Senses. It is not enough to let our minds do the teaching and learning. Whether it be seeing, touching, smelling, tasting—these are all gateways to learning that should not be ignored both for children and older persons. Whether it be some highly developed sense of intellect or good old barnyard common sense, all of these sensitivities can contribute. Visual aids depend on these gates to teach. The more pathways we can follow into the lives of persons, the more effective our teaching can be.

Use Surroundings to Teach. The classroom teaches. So can the city street or the country pasture. Furniture in your classroom, colors, temperatures, seating arrangements, lighting, windows, work space—all these contribute to the discipline of teaching. So also does the general climate you and your students together create. How you talk with each other, the respect and caring you show, the mood you develop from quiet and reflective to enthusiastic and outgoing—these are co-teachers through bulletin boards and items that you bring into the room. Even the way you dress makes some contribution.

Model What You Want Learned. Teachers and fellow learners offer a living example to other students. The ways we teach students will often be the ways those same learners will use in teaching others later on. Whatever the form, a concept or an ethic or a plan is acted out in front of learners and from this class members learn how they can do it for themselves.

Provide for Repetition and Reinforcement. Some things we learn by doing over and over again until we have developed a skill. We do want to beware of practicing our mistakes over and over again until they are totally ingrained. This approach says that it doesn't hurt to repeat great Bible stories and to use central Bible teaching repeatedly—so long as we do this deliberately, with both eyes open and one eye looking out for the boring. The great Bible teachings bear repeating at regular intervals throughout a person's life.

It is also good to reinforce positive learning with good support, compliments, and encouragement. It may be debatable whether positive reinforcement in the form of rewards for good learning behavior and negative reinforcement in the form of punishment for poor learning behavior are valid. Generally good learning should be its own reward.

Support Learning through Association. Learning is supported through the process of association for everyone and particularly for adults whose rote learning skills may have faded a bit.

Learning is speeded when one is able to relate some new idea or fact to other more familiar elements. It helps to be able to put new things in a meaningful old framework. We sometimes use this to remember a person's name. Maybe you have just met Mrs. White and note that she has on a beautiful white coat. But watch out if the next time you meet her she has on a beautiful purple coat.

Use Basic Learning Tools Such as Memorization. Basic reading and writing help us learn. The person who cannot read with some ease and skill and understanding is handicapped in many kinds of learning. It is good for the church, a people of the Book, to support the continued growth and development of reading skills throughout the life span. Among other basic learning skills is the ancient and honorable approach of memorization. This was at one time the principal mode of storage of information, but the development and spread of writing, reading, and modern media—especially present-day computer technology—has made memory seem less important. But it is still a worthy skill and one to be cultivated. It does need to be used in meaningful and appropriate and inviting ways.

Support Learning through Creative Expression. There is something about creativity that is very close to God. To allow learners to give creative expression to the concepts and facts they are dealing with fosters reflection and encourages communication. The making of things according to patterns and rigid instructions is perhaps good craftsmanship but is not creativity. Music, artwork, writing—such methods as these springing out of creative expression can help learners sharpen their grasp of the ideas with which they are grappling.

Dialogue Aids Learning. When mind meets mind, when several open-minded seekers after truth are in communication with each other, real learning is likely to take place. This is discussion with a plus. It involves people really leveling with one another and making sure they understand and are understood. The spirit of dialogue provides the wings by which an ordinary time of discussion can be turned into a genuine sharing, learning experience. It works on the assumption that differences of view are good and desirable. It assumes an atmosphere that permits, indeed values, confrontation with respect and under critical discipline.

74

Learning Thrives on Problem-Solving. Too often we just list, catalog, dramatize, picture, worry about, and broadcast our problems. Basic to learning is facing up realistically to problems and then working to solve them. Sometimes this takes place through case studies, sometimes through acting out, sometimes through a variety of discussion procedures. A healthy approach to learning assumes that the learner has problems, has the right to make mistakes, and can be encouraged to work on those in a highly unique and individual way.

To Learn, Use One's Own Words. It is a test of learning and indeed a means of carrying out that learning to put others' viewpoints and ideas into our own words. This may involve us in writing, paraphrasing, dramatizing, and role playing. A test of whether or not we actually understand something is this: Can we put it into our own words and explain it well to someone else?

Learn through Research. Research involves a complex of exploratory procedures that are helpful in learning. This approach draws together reading, engaging in disciplined study, using various tools to reach new insights. Then as research is reported communication with others becomes a part of the picture, itself a useful aspect of learning.

Use Evaluation to Learn. Have we met our goals? What actually have we done? The research needed to provide this picture and the basis for making an estimate of our accomplishments involve a cluster of significant learning approaches. Reflection on the learning process is helpful. This can result in improved procedures in the future. Testing in written and oral forms may be involved here, even in church related situations. Feedback is indeed an important aspect of teaching. Through it all, however, we should be at work to build up self-esteem and not to damage one's confidence and sense of competence.

These are but some of the basic learning skills that could be mentioned here. Together they add up to a checklist of approaches to learning that any teacher should be using in a balanced way. They involve skills that all those who would teach share a responsibility for fostering. They lead on to the specific learning methods or activities that will be discussed in the next chapter.

We Like to Learn in Differing Ways

Learners are different kinds of people. They have differing preferences about how they do their learning. Teachers have preferences for different styles of teaching. One teacher feels most comfortable in a discussion, another with giving a lecture. One student may actually learn best in a reflective mood while another may learn most efficiently by doing something.

These differences have practical implications for teachers:

1. Knowledge of the preferred learning styles of students would be helpful so that teaching efforts can be adjusted to take into account their strongest preferences.

2. Likewise, knowing the current preferences of students will increase balance in learning procedures. For example, students might prefer a passive, reflective style of learning, yet for the sake of their total learning need to be helped to make greater use of and find more satisfaction in active approaches. Or, the opposite might be true.

3. Teachers need to be aware of their own position on the spectrum of possible learning styles. Perhaps they will find they have a hobby of using one approach, whereas other approaches might better serve their particular students or content. The teacher may need to offer a more balanced menu for teaching.

The general direction for teaching/learning styles indicated here starts with awareness of where we are as teachers in our learning preferences and how those match with the learning preferences of our particular students. But we are not just interested in status quo and matching students and learners. We are in the long range most interested in effective learning styles rather than in just fitting into comfortable ruts. Sometimes learning styles need to be broadened and changed. We are not always to be concerned simply with selling our educational wares to the student market as it now exists. Changes may be in order on either side.

But exactly what are the common learning preferences? Educational research has helped us learn about these by describing four dimensions of learning and four categories of learners.[1] Precise information about where we stand in these areas can be arrived at through testing, but many of us can get a fairly accurate picture of ourselves and individual students by simple observation and reflection.

Let's look, for example, at how many people learn to bowl. They tend to start out simply by rolling the ball down the lane. That is a learning activity that focuses on doing. The bowlers stand at the line and observe what happens. A split? A strike? Maybe a gutter ball.

Then they may think about what they have done. They may reflect on how they held the ball and the steps they took before releasing the ball. Here is a learning activity that focuses on observation and reflection.

As a third step the new bowler may take the time to consult a neighboring, more experienced bowler who has been watching the entire event up to now. What did I do wrong? How should I make my approach? Did I twist my wrist? How do the good bowlers go about all of this? Some research is carried out. Some theorizing about good bowling is done. This third learning activity involves some abstract development of concepts.

As a fourth step the new bowler may again pick up the ball, practice holding it this way and that, even try out balls with different finger holes. The bowler may practice approaching the line, may go through all the motions without releasing the ball. In this fourth learning activity he or she is actively experimenting.

Finally, the bowler once again rolls the ball down the alley. Maybe this time or soon—a strike!

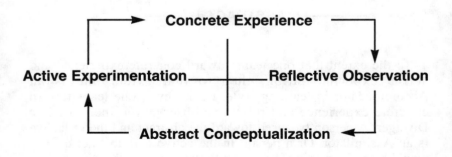

The four stages this bowler went through represent a cycle that we all experience in learning a sport or other skill. Actually, we may enter the cycle at any point and conclude it at any point. Or, we may have our favorite spot along the cycle where we prefer to stay, something that is more possible in some fields than bowling. Note the crossing lines in this diagram.[2]

You can reflect on your own experience and preferences and place yourself just by a sense of judgment along the lines at two points. Where do you mark yourself on the horizontal line between the active and reflective? Where on the vertical line between the concrete and the abstract? You can make the same estimate of your students.

The spotting of yourself on the continuums can also locate you in one of four learning preference areas. Draw lines at the right angles from the two points on the continuums in a direction so that they will intersect. The area in which they intersect indicates a learning preference in one of four areas. The areas:

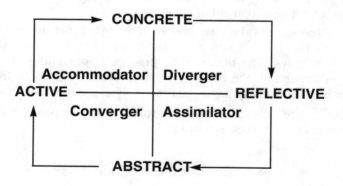

To the extent that one leans toward concrete experience and active experimentation, then to that extent one is an Accommodator in learning style. If, however, one leans toward concrete experience and reflective observation, then one is a Diverger. A person balanced toward the abstract and the reflective is an Assimilator. Or a person in the active and abstract quarter would be a Converger. The nearer to the center of the diagram the testing places a person, the more open that person would normally be to other styles of teaching and learning. We are not forced to stay in one pigeonhole, and as teachers we can exercise our approaches in all four areas in order to foster a balanced learning approach.

Just what is involved in the learning approaches of these four areas? Let's examine some of the possibilities.

The Accommodator, who roams that area between concrete experience and active experimentation, is obviously most happy when learning involves doing things. This kind of person likes new experiences, lots of variety, even some risk-taking in the learning process. The Accommodator is more impressed by facts than by theories and will go for what appears to be precise data over generalized observations and broad perceptions. This person is likely to proceed rather intuitively involving problems, working at them in trial-and-error style. Such persons are often in sales fields. They may prefer to receive packaged information rather than think their way inductively into new insights. There are, of course, many admirable qualities in being an Accommodator-Teacher-Learner. Many teachers in the church are of this style. So are many learners.

The Converger (between Active Experimentation and Concrete Experience) loves to make practical applications of ideas. This kind of teacher or learner likes to find, in rather unemotional, often detached style, a single right answer to a question. Often this person is detached from other persons, is more concerned with ideas, processes, and especially things.

Such a person prefers to learn by engaging in projects, doing very clearly spelled out individual assignments, or at most working with a few other persons in small groups. Lecturing, particularly on broad and general topics, is not usually welcome. Convergers often have rather technical interests and like to be approached in some relationship to those. They may be engineers or mechanics or cooks. Many church school teachers and learners fall into this category.

The Assimilator generally uses strong mental capacities to reflect on situations and develop abstract conceptions of the world around her or him. This kind of person places high value on the analytical and rational approaches and develops critical thinking habits. In areas in which such a person is highly motivated the Assimilator prefers efficient ways to learn—for him or her—that come through lectures, reading, and research. Such a person is concerned with basic sciences and mathematics, for example, rather than the applied sciences. The name assimilator comes because these people are able to take widely different observations and bodies of thought and bring them together in meaningful new combinations.

The Diverger is able to take the concrete and deal with it reflectively. Such people are often characterized by a strong imaginative ability. They are good at idea generation. They are involved with the arts and they are people-oriented. Many times they prefer relating to peers rather than to authorities. They may be able to tolerate more ambiguity and deal with uncertainties to a greater extent than persons in the other three categories. Such people tend to be counselors. They may be focused educationally on the liberal arts.

TEACHING ON THE AGE LEVELS

Notes to Teachers of Early Childhood

Phyllis G., longtime teacher of third graders in the church, writes: "I've gone through different moods and expectations of children during the twenty years I've taught these youngsters. At first, I felt I simply had to let them play for a while, which I thought was just so much wasted time as far as my teaching was concerned. Then I would try to get them together and quiet for a few minutes of real teaching in which I would try to pass along nuggets from the Word of God as long as I could force them to sit still. Then off they would go romping again.

"In my second phase I was almost forced to give up on my formal teaching attempts. I just tried to help them have a good time, and I would wind up feeling like a baby sitter.

"Now things have moved on for me into something more constructive. I feel comfortable with some play—which I find a meaningful, informal teaching time. Then there is time for a story. Time for the children to be quietly involved in interest centers, time for singing and playing rhythm band together. Just a variety of things that I try to make meaningful.

"I had to accept that the learning style of these children was action-oriented and experiential."

Studying this chapter in light of early childhood: How would your own testimony of working with pre-school children be like this teacher? How different? Think with your peers about the preferred learning styles of young children? What part does socialization, association, the disciplines of learning play in their lives? Write your own teacher's testimony about how you have found it to be effective in teaching this age level. If you are just looking at this age level as a possibility for teaching, you might gather a testimony or so about teaching young children from experienced teachers and examine those for clues about these children as learners.

Notes to Teachers of Elementary Children

Here is a recollection by a teacher of upper elementary children as learners. "I've usually found the children in this class pretty eager to learn—really learn, that is. They like to be given a challenge. They like for the assignments to be clear and definite. They like for things to be interesting. The good readers thoroughly like to read. Some of the boys and girls get real satisfaction out of memorizing. Of course, some of them like to talk and try getting us off the subject.

Some complain about things being so much like school, but down underneath they seem to get along better under a fairly disciplined approach than one that is too vague and free.

"Now I do have to say that my fifth graders are more the way I have been talking than my sixth graders. Those older kids are getting restless and tired of being associated with a class or department they associate with children. They're on the threshold of adolescence, and things are beginning to change for them.

There's a lot of difference, really, in teaching in this department. Some read as well as any adult you know. The same goes for writing. They may be better at lettering and making posters than their parents. But others—I don't know. Some can hardly read at all. Some regard my classroom as a prison. Some kids are good at everything, some good at games but not classroom stuff. Some are pretty naive, others are shrewd.

"Some can talk up an intellectual storm. Most are pretty nice but others are smart alecks. Some you would think are so sophisticated that they know or can deal with just about any subject on earth until you scratch beneath the surface enough to find out they still are children with all the limitations of children's understandings. Teaching them is both fun and challenge!"

Studying this chapter in light of elementary childhood: If you have been teaching this age child, how would your own experience of their learning compare with this recollection? How would it be different? Think with your peers about the preferred learning styles of elementary children.

What part do such learning skills as reading, writing, research, experimentation, and memorization play in their learning? Write your own teacher's testimony of how you have found children to be as learners in this age level. Or if you have not taught in the area, write down your expectations. Compare these with other teachers.

Notes to Teachers of Youth

Jack T. has been a church worker with youth for three years. When he was asked how he regarded them as learners he described them to us:

"It's amazing to me how dumb and how smart these kids can be—all on the same subject and almost on the same day. They can be very shrewd, figuring things out, putting things together. They know a lot, and they can figure out a lot. They learn easily. Oh, some are growing so fast they run out of energy quickly. Some just don't concentrate. They are often so interested in each other in a class that they don't concentrate on what I'm trying to teach them very well. It's usually when they're hyper about something else going on with them or in their group that they start looking dumb to me. Those differences in the kids have been one of my problems.

"For some, a lot of the biblical material and other things we're dealing with in class is old stuff. They may even think of that as kid's stuff. Other youth, sometimes new to the group or sometimes on the slower side, aren't ready to go as fast as I'd like to go. We have all kinds.

"Generally, I find that if I can grab their attention with a live issue close to their everyday world to start with, then we can move on bringing the Christian faith to bear on that in good style. Most of the time they are ready for tougher stuff than I often wind up giving them. I want to keep them interested, but sometimes the way to do that is to offer tough challenges more than just easy material that is entertaining.

"They do get disrupted in their learning process by all the things that are cooking in their lives, and I have to take that into account. I try to work on a basis that helps them really know who they are and to appreciate themselves for that. Being adolescents with all its changes is a handicap for learning, but also a gateway."

Studying this chapter in light of youth: If you have worked with youth, how would your testimony about them as learners differ from this youth observation? With what do you agree the most? Discuss this with your peers. What part do such academic disciplines as reading, memorizing, and writing play in your work with youth? What is the importance of socialization and formal study? If you have not taught youth yet, what do you anticipate in this area? Maybe you could write out your own expectation of youth as learners.

Notes to Teachers of Adults

Adrian H. has grown older with an adult class he started teaching when its members were in their twenties, and now they are in their upper forties and fifties. How has he experienced the learning process in adults?

"It's interesting to me that my class has changed so much in what it wants to talk about across these twenty years. At first, they wanted to spend a lot of time talking about their small children and how to raise them. Sometimes, they wanted to get into marital issues. There was some talk about their jobs, getting ahead, getting along on little money. Now, of course, we talk about grandchildren, but we seem to spend more time on broad world issues, biblical teachings, and the like.

"But all the way through, I've found I've had to stay close to what the class felt was relevant and important to their lives right then. If we strayed very far from that, they told me about it. Always they seemed to want to bring in their experience to apply to the situation, and we have increasingly varied experiences to deal with.

"The class doesn't seem quite as ready to do a variety of learning activities as they used to. Maybe they are just a little more forward in giving me the sign that they don't want to try too many new classroom activities and they don't want to be put on the spot with active participation. Oh, they love to discuss. That is at the heart of what we do. I'm getting concerned that they would rather talk about religion than do very much about it.

"The way some of them like to learn in class becomes more and more pronounced all the time. Some do prefer to be active. Others like to be more theoretical. Some like to put together old and new ideas as well as theory with possible action and see where things come out. It all adds up that I still try to use a variety of approaches to try to keep everybody happy. I have a hard time getting many of them to study or prepare anything outside of class. And they won't give a thought to memorizing anything, but we keep working at it."

Studying this chapter in light of adulthood: What would be your own testimony about the learning style and approach of adults? You yourself being an adult, what helps you best to learn? What are your main concerns in learning—approaches you prefer to make in class, problems for learning that you experience, joys you find in some ways of going about it? Think with your peers about adults as learners and write your own statement describing adults as learners. Take into account statements in the previous testimony that you especially agree or disagree with. What special guidelines for understanding the adult as a learner would you follow? In what ways are adults more effective or less effective learners than younger persons? How do young, middle, and older adults differ from each other in their learning interests and capacities?

STUDYING THIS CHAPTER IN CLASS

Possible Goals
- To become acquainted with what learning means and how it gets carried out through various learning tasks.

- To survey some of the basic learning approaches and skills that are appropriate means of getting at the learning tasks.

A Class Plan
1. Ask students to identify which learning tasks were being called for in the eight class situations described in the beginning of Chapter 3. (See the section in this chapter. Learning tasks can be applied to what was going on in those eight situations in Chapter 3 somewhat as follows: A, discovery; B, exploring, perhaps some appropriating personally; C, exploring and discovery; D, exploring and discovery; E, listening, perhaps exploring; F, a mixture with emphasis on exploring and discovering; G, exploring; H, becoming convinced and acting on convictions. Note that the umbrella task of listening and responding would appear everywhere.)

2. List on the chalkboard and rate importance of some basic skills that learning generally calls for. (This is a list of learning tasks or approaches that appears in the text under Learning Skills (p. 67). Ask students, perhaps working by small groups of three or four, to examine the list and rate the items in accordance with their importance. They could star those they think most basic, put a minus by any they feel should be minimized. Then share and discuss in the total group.)

3. Discover which of the skills are called for in the eight classroom situations in Chapter 3. (Note which skills are being called for. Mark any heavy use of any one particular skill. Discuss why some skills may not have shown up in our sample.)

Notes

1. Wide-ranging study of learning styles and preferences has been carried out in recent years. I am indebted for the terminology employed here to David Kolb in *An Experiential Learning Theory* (1984) and *Organizational Psychology* (1984).

The *Learning Style Inventory* is copyrighted by David A. Kolb. Both are distributed by McBer and Co., 116 Huntington Ave, Boston, Mass 02116. The booklet contains further information on theory, construction, reliability, and validity of the inventory and is available from McBer in packets of ten at $65 per packet (1995 pricing).

2. As developed by Kurt Lewin.

And these words which I command you this day shall be upon your heart; and you shall teach them diligently to your children, and shall talk of them when you sit in your house, and when you walk by the way, and when you lie down, and when you rise. And you shall bind them as a sign upon your hand, and they shall be a frontlets between your eyes. And you shall write them on the doorposts of your house and on your gates.

—Deuteronomy 6:6–9

Chapter 5

Bridges to Learning Activities

- *Why can't I just tell 'em the truth? That ought to be good enough.*
- *What are the secrets of having a good discussion? of being a good storyteller?*
- *How can you tell if you have chosen a good teaching method?*

Somebody in a class one time asked, "About how many good teaching activities are there?" And I replied, "Three hundred sixty-five." Some people took that in all seriousness. Actually my 365 came from the number of days in the year and was intended to suggest that there are a vast number of possible activities and at least enough to use a different one every day.

In fact, I tried to teach that college class for a semester without repeating in exactly the same fashion any one teaching activity. But the important thing is not how many different methods we can use to teach but how well we use each one of them and what their effectiveness is in communicating the gospel. How well do they bridge between the student and the good news of Jesus Christ?

Jesus himself used a wide variety of teaching methods. Those ranged from telling parables, asking open-ended, thought-provoking questions, engaging in one-to-one dialogues, using visual aids like shepherds and sheep and coins. Our list could go on and on.

Or go back to a Jewish home a couple of hundred years before Christ and note the different methods used to carry out the teaching responsibility given that family in Deuteronomy and elsewhere.

In one corner of the house the mother instructs her daughter in mending some of the family clothes. She demonstrates and then the little girl plies the needle and thread under her mother's watchful eye. In an attached room the father, a leather worker, scrapes the hide of a goat and shows his young son how to work with it. As the two of them come from the workshed into the house they touch the Mezuzah on the door post and kiss the finger that has touched that container reminding them all of the Shema, that keystone Hebrew scripture passage found in Deuteronomy 6:4: "Hear, O Israel, the Lord our God is one Lord." The father wears a phylactery bound to his forehead and the mother wears one on her arm. These carry the same Shema and other scriptures that are basic in their lives. Every child is taught diligently what these passages mean.

They can look down the road where in the distance they see a pile of large stones. The son asks why those stones are piled up in that odd way. The father explains that this is a memorial reminding them of the time when their ancestors occupied this land so that the Israelites could return to the land they felt God promised them.

And in the evening the family, together with their grandfather and grandmother and others who lived with them, will climb the stairs to sit on the flat roof and catch the evening breeze under the stars. Then grandfather will start telling stories of how God has dealt faithfully across the years with their people. Many are exciting adventure stories. At times also the son will recite the Bible passage he learned in synagogue school that day from reading in the scripture scroll.

So it was that the ancient Hebrew family taught. We could come on down to the one-room schoolhouses that were built everywhere along the American frontier. One teacher would use many devices to teach ten or fifteen children ranging across the first eight grades. Much use of personal study and research. Older students teaching the younger ones. Drawing pictures to illustrate the ABCs. Holding spelldowns. Learning poetry. Reading in McGuffy's. Solving problems. Telling stories. The list goes on and on.

And so our heritage in both religious and public education reflects a wide variety of teaching activities to use wherever education was taking place. Think back to the Israelite home, for example. We find there the parents modeling the faith and the Hebrew way of life before their children in everyday life. We find direct teaching through the demonstration and practice of skills. We find peers helping each other to know. Conversations and dialogues are taking place. Great stories of faith are being told. We see the result of reading and memorizing being put into practice. We see the use of visual aids in the phylacteries and mezuzahs and the memorial stones. The Book of Deuteronomy directly urges the use of many of these devices. It seemed to be well understood that teaching the faith called for the use of a wide variety of activities. Our call to teach today suggests that we are to come at the teaching role with the use of a similar variety of methods. These need to be effective, appropriate, and attractive to both teacher and learner.

Some Learning Situations

Let's look at some random happenings in classes, just to get in mind a variety of the kinds of things that do take place. You may react positively to some, negatively to others.

1. It is an adult Sunday school class of about a dozen. One person reads a verse of the lesson's Bible passage for the day. The next person reads a note about it from the commentary section of the student handbook. Then the next Bible reader takes the following verse, and so on. Every once in a while the teacher adds a comment. "We have done this every Sunday since I joined the class six years ago," one student tells us.

2. It looks like playtime in the kindergarten room at church. Over in one corner three or four boys and girls are busy at the housekeeping center. There are toy stoves, small tables and chairs, dolls, and the like. In another corner girls and boys are playing with hammers and pieces of wood in a workshop setting. Elsewhere we see a pet hamster and a row of tiny young plants.

3. The youth class is trying to have a discussion. But it does not seem to be going too well. After asking several questions that nobody answers, the teacher resorts to calling on several students. The teacher gets a few very brief responses, which are labeled as either right or wrong

4. A learning game is going on in the upper elementary class. It is fun and calls for considerable moving around. The youngsters get carried away and really make a lot of noise. Their class meets in a fellowship hall area with folding accordion doors along one side. The other side is open to the middle of the large room. Other classes are noticing all the laughing and scuffling. At the end of the activity, however, one boy says, "That really was fun! I wish Sunday school was like this all the time. And I learned something today I never knew before."

Some of these learning activities are obviously working out better than others. Some bring good results but cause problems along the way. Some are good activities being carried out poorly. Some are of very limited usefulness to start with. Several guideline questions may be asked of these and any other classroom learning activities we might think of. They are the sorts of questions you can ask of any methods you find suggested in your teaching resources or that occur to you as you plan to lead a session.

Checklist for Learning Activities

1. Does this method support the students in learning for themselves?

Some learning activities do everything for the student. They simply help the teacher transmit some bit of knowledge. If we believe, however, that each learner must do learning for himself or herself, that is, engage in learning tasks, then we would give highest priority to those learning activities that call for the learner to be active rather than passive. This favors activities that call for meaningful student participation—projects, problem-solving, acting out situations. These would be favored more than simply looking at pictures or hearing lectures.

Such an approach, of course, does not rule out those more passive activities because when they are well done and when a student is actively interested, the student may be inwardly but still actively responding. This does mean that those activities that call for a student to explore and discover rather than just receive from a teacher would rank highest on our list. Some learning activities that are strong here include these:

Role playing

Service projects

Guided research

Learning games

Some of these learning activities that are not so strong at this point:

Listening to a cassette

Listening to a lecture

Looking at a picture that completely tells the story

Hearing someone read from the student handbook

2. Does the learning activity advance the session purpose and the general objective?

Is it on the subject? Does it have serious purpose? Is it a genuine contribution to learning, or is it merely interesting? Does it help the learner change in the direction of the purpose, or is it simply something that interests the teacher? Is it too vaguely related to the purpose to be obvious to the learners that this is a purposeful activity? Some activities detour too far in their efforts to interest, amuse, and intrigue learners.

3. Is it appropriate to the time, place, and facilities?

A reading activity is not going to work with nonreaders. An

approach that constantly focuses around reading is not going to be successful in the long run with a group of marginal readers. So an activity that calls for skills that are beyond most of these class members simply isn't going to work too well. Nor, on the other hand, is an activity that learners perceive to be too juvenile for them. An adult class might at first resist a fingerpainting activity unless it is presented to them in humor or unless they see its relevance for them. Very active and noisy games are not appropriate in crowded facilities where classes are close together. Activities should take into account how students are dressed. Projects that do not fit into the normal class schedule need to be evaluated in light of time available.

4. Is the method interesting? fun? Is it different from the routine?

More people are turned away from the Kingdom by the dullness of its representatives than by all the powers of evil. Classes don't have to be dull, even though there is one theory—going all the way back to Aristotle—that we don't learn anything without some degree of pain. Our task is to be bright and interesting, to share joy in learning. The learning activity needs to be attention-getting and pleasurable enough that learners want to stay with it.

Variety is both the spice of life and the spice of a classroom. Just because one thing works well for a teacher is no reason for it to take place every week. A teaching plan that is basically the same pattern week after week may simplify things for the teacher but complicate the work of being really interesting and helpful.

5. Is this activity meaningful? more than busywork?

All too often a method does look like mere busywork. That can be true when the teacher has pulled in something farfetched to use in the classroom without relating it to the session. This can happen when the purpose of the session is not clearly kept in sight. This can happen when the teacher finds particular methods enjoyable and fun but doesn't relate them to the session. Handwork activities for younger children sometimes fall into this category. The activity should directly and obviously relate.

6. Does this activity relate students to others, especially other students, in a meaningful way?

We don't usually learn much inside a vacuum. We live in a world of people. Particularly the concepts that we find significant in the church benefit from being explored and developed in a setting with other people. It is good if an exploring group together can come up with shared insights. This reinforces learners in their own discoveries. It adds to mutual strength in acting on what has been learned. Learners are often more open to learning from their own age-group peers than from an older teacher and from outside resource material.

Reading by oneself and doing private research obviously have a place in the scheme of things. Yet reports on reading and research usually need to be shared for the full benefit to accrue to the reader or researcher. Learning centers, with all the many things that are in their favor, would be unworthy learning activities if they were used exclusively and if some of their activities did not involve the learner with others. For many people solitary learning is a slow, tedious, and often unrewarding process.

7. Is this method worth the time, effort, and cost?

We all serve with some limits on the time we can spend, the effort we can put out, and the budget under which we operate. A method that produces a small result might be worth a small effort and minimum cost. But so often the very things that cost the most money wind up being least effective in the classroom. There is a stewardship to be exercised in the classroom. There is a stewardship to be exercised here. It is, for instance, hardly worth the teacher's time to fix up elaborate cutouts for each kindergarten child.

8. Is this method honest and not manipulative?

If anybody ought to be honest with students it should be a teacher representing the church. A good activity ought to be presented in straightforward fashion with its purpose usually clearly understood "We are doing this today because…." The end does not justify just any old means. We want learners to engage in a study enthusiastically because they fully recognize what they can gain from this activity and that's what they want to gain. If we are going to use an activity that does have some tricky twist to it, probably it is well to warn the students that something like this is in the offing. Then we can see if they still want to participate.

9. Does this activity avoid putting individual students under undue pressure and embarrassment?

Our world offers enough pressures and embarrassments to start with. Far be it from the Sunday church school to add unnecessarily to that list. Life seems to hand us enough win-lose situations that we don't need to perpetuate that kind of pressure in the classroom. Thus, wisdom would dictate that we avoid activities that in any large and significant ways make winners out of some in the class and losers out of the rest. Cooperation on a mutual project is generally better than a competitive approach. For this reason many teachers avoid asking point-blank questions with fact level answers because they see no need to apply this kind of pressure. Instead they seek volunteers. Or, if they ask questions directly to an individual they limit their inquiries to matters in which each answerer has a right to a personal opinion. If certain roles in a dramatic situation would embarrass the student player, avoid assigning them to such a student.

10. Does the activity appeal to the highest and the best motivations?

Motivations lie within us. They are purposes that are all our own which we seek to fulfill in order to achieve some sort of satisfaction or fill some need. People from outside cannot give us motivations, but they can stimulate those we have. Some teachers pick up activities they feel or have been told will "motivate" the learner. Others have learned that they can encourage, stimulate, or feed certain motivations that already exist.

The idea is to stimulate the good motivations and leave the others alone. Activities can do that. They can appeal to the best in us or to the not-so-good. Some activities can feed on jealously, greed, selfishness—not so good! Others can be based on a person's faith, hope, generosity, or helpfulness. The wise teacher will check out learning activities for that.

11. Does the activity support balanced use of the appropriate basic learning approaches?

These include means of learning such as repetition and reinforcement, association, experiencing, reflection, creative expression. Note some of the basic learning approaches mentioned in Chapter 4. Over a period of time the types of learning activities used in a class should draw upon most if not all of these. Together these form a symphony for learning involving a wide variety of instruments tuned to each other and conducted in close coordination. If a person is not ready for a given activity, then that activity shouldn't be used with such a learner. If we believe people learn much through socialization, through dialogue with others, through following models, then we seek for them to learn through ways that use these approaches.

Some Basic Teaching Activities

Out of hundreds of teaching activity possibilities, we present here a few basic ones. We are not trying to be comprehensive but to indicate a range of possibilities, each with advantages for certain kinds of situations and disadvantages for others. It is helpful for teachers to have a range of methods in mind and for them not to be slaves to the particular activities a printed resource might suggest.

Discussion

Some form of conversation is basic to teaching across all age levels. By the time learners move into youth and adult years, they are involved more and more in discussion as a classroom activity. Some rules for good discussion are these:

1. Don't simply pool your ignorance; arrange for ways to introduce helpful content into the discussion.

2. Most of the time discussion will center on issues, on concerns, and concepts rather than facts. This means asking questions that

don't have quick yes or no answers. If you are seeking to communicate information, use another activity.

3. Seek wide participation in the discussion. Don't let this be conversation that goes from teacher to student and back to teacher without involving many students in a free flow and interchange of ideas. Don't allow one or two people to dominate a discussion.

4. Plan basic discussion questions carefully to get more than yes or no answers. Plan to move toward a goal through the discussion.

5. Help the class see what progress is being made by summing up frequently where they are and suggesting directions in which they need now to move.

In light of this checklist, using discussion has an advantage in that it involves the students actively, usually in stating for themselves where they are in light of the subject. It allows the teacher to step back and set the stage for student exploration.

An obvious disadvantage of discussion is that it can turn out to be a mere sharing of ignorance if nobody has real content to bring to it. It can fail to involve a large number. It can be an easy substitute for a variety of activities that can get class members deeply involved. Mere questions and answers can be seen as a substitute for genuine discussion. Many learners simply talk about the issue at hand instead of doing anything about it.

Storytelling

This activity takes place at all levels and in all kinds of places—in the kindergarten circle, in the pulpit, in the college lecture hall. As a master teacher Jesus himself employed it with his parables. The activity has several essential ingredients—a cracking good story line, elements with which hearers can identify, skill on the part of the storyteller.

It's best if the story can really be told, not just read casually out of a piece of resource material. It's better if real conversation can be maintained. There is a basic simplicity in most good stories. The story needs to have a point appropriate to the session. Eye contact between the teller and those hearing the story is important.

There are many forms of specific activity that storytelling can take. In addition to the teacher-teller, a story can be told on a film-strip or video. It can be read from a book. It can be acted out. Some suggestions for storytelling are these:

1. Choose the story carefully.

2. Tell the story well.

3. Tell the story with animation, enthusiasm, and eye contact with the hearers.

4. Don't moralize; let the story make its own point.

5. Don't forget that adults learn from and like stories, too.

Among disadvantages are the following:

1. Better no story at all than a poor story poorly told.

2. Listeners may derive the wrong point, or they may get lost in details and lose the main idea.

3. We may easily be too moralizing and therefore in the long run ineffective.

4. A story that is repeated too often in routine fashion has nega-tive results.

Small-group Work

Involvement and personal decision making may be increased in classes of six or more by the use of small groups. Students may work in pairs, thirds, quads, or larger small groups. Sometimes tongues are loosened and thought is stimulated when we start out a discussion with some neighbor nudging between pairs of students who happen to be sitting beside each other.

Some people also are able to express themselves in a group of five or six when they would rarely speak before fifteen or twenty-five.

Small groups can perform a variety of functions. They can be formed to carry out projects. They can be responsible for varying phases of the total class session. They can deal with a variety of discussion questions and bring back a contribution to the discus-sion of the total group.

In an approach sometimes referred to as buzz grouping, the large class moves back and forth from total group into buzz groups of six to twelve, where a convener and a recorder are assigned. Given a limited question and kept under time pressure, the various buzz groups in the room deal with the same issue and report back their range of replies to it.

One growing approach to small group life goes under the name of Cooperative Learning. Here students work together in small, fixed groups on a structured learning task. The group works on an assigned task over a period of time. Students learn primarily from each other, but they are assisted by a teacher who acts as a mentor and facilitator. A sense of both individual independence and group interdependence is fostered. Through it all positive cooperation in moving toward a set of learning goals is sought.

Small group work has several advantages:

1. It encourages ideas and deeper participation in discussion and problem solving.

2. It allows for variety and change of pace in larger classes.

3. It allows for the stimulation and strength of a larger class group while also providing intimacy and direct personal involvement in a smaller group.

Disadvantages include these:

1. Some learners are threatened by being put into small groups and seek to avoid such situations.

2. Physical facilities in some churches do not allow this to be done readily, although small groups can be formed even where there are fixed pews. Noise may distract other classes.

3. Some students do not hear one another well in a classroom full of talk.

4. When carried out rigidly and mechanically, small groups may be dead and ineffective.

5. If a class group is already small, further dividing may not pay any special dividends.

6. Occasionally some personalities will clash when closely tied together. A poor learning climate may be created by that.

Valuing Process

One group of methods clusters around approaches that help students identify, clarify, and confront values—the matters they voluntarily commit themselves to as important in their lives. In this approach, some issue, stand, or concern is presented to the class members. They then make some open declaration about where they personally stand in relation to it. Through various devices learners are asked to put themselves on the line regarding it. They have to think it through and decide how important it is to them.

Typical valuing activities include the following: (a) Voting. The students raise their hands or make some other public commitment to one side or other of a given belief or position. (b) Marking a continuum. The students judge where they stand individually on an issue that extends on a line from one extreme to another. (c) Taking a position on an area of the floor marked for strong agreement or disagreement with statement of value. (d) Assigning weight, importance, or value in varying degrees to a range of views. For example, learners may bid in an auction or budget for an imaginary expense in valuing games.

Advantages

1. Valuing approaches force us to think things through and to take a public stand for what we decide we most want to believe. We are forced to clarify and strengthen our convictions.

2. Valuing causes learning to involve searching and being active.

3. The approach calls for individual responsibility and commitment.

Disadvantages

1. The crowd may be unduly influential in the choice-making.

2. The approach does not in itself provide information about the choice-making; its emphasis is upon what one already believes deep down inside.

3. The methodology may be overused with some pupils, considering both their church and school experience.

4. Valuing may tend to make beliefs and practices look relative rather than fixed, an approach with both strengths and weaknesses.

Memorization

Far less emphasis is placed on this method by general education these days than in an earlier era before inexpensive printed copies and computers put sources at our fingertips. And yet memorization is a significant learning tool. It provides data on which the mind can work readily. The multiplication of modern Bible translations complicates the Bible memorization process, but it is still important for those who would live by the Bible to carry significant parts of it with them in their minds.

Memorization should always be carried out in ways that insure it will have real meaning for the learner. There is no good reason to memorize passages without relevance to the learner. There should be real value in the work for the learner, other than memorizing for prizes, for recognition, or out of peer-group pressure. Sheer memorization drill or routine week-after-week approaches are not too helpful despite the air of sacredness some persons have attached to this learning tool.

Advantages

1. Memorization forces us to give disciplined and careful attention to Bible and other material that is to be memorized.

2. It is sometimes important to have the material to be memorized readily available to us without referral to books and other sources.

3. The method fits in with and enhances other basic learning approaches.

Disadvantages

1. Memorization can be carried on without sufficient attention to meaning and readiness of learners.

2. Memorization can be a substitute for other approaches that help the learners know how to think and make decisions and other important aspects of their discipleship.

3. Memorization can foster a kind of rote approach to the Christian faith on the level of knowing facts but without emphasis on understanding and applying Christian principles.

Audio–Visual Aids

Learning needs to be approached through all the avenues that lead us into a person's mind and feelings. The spoken word alone is not enough. The written word alone is not enough. Increasing emphasis is placed these days on a visual approach. We realize more about the importance of a multimedia approach involving sight, sound, and other gates to the heart and mind.

Along with this comes a wave of equipment, devices, and technologies. Video equipment, audio cassette tape players, filmstrip and slide projectors, instant cameras, camcorders and other photography equipment are a few kinds readily available. Computer technology and other aspects of the information superhighway loom larger year by year. There are record players, bulletin boards, turnover charts, chalkboards, and handcraft materials of all kinds.

All of them can be useful in gaining attention and in making things clear. The title of the general category here needs to be kept in mind, of course—these are aids and not the central part of the learning process. They can foster. They can assist.

Most curriculum materials suggest ways and means of enhancing class sessions through the use of various kinds of audio-visual aids. Many established curriculum series offer resource kits each quarter correlating with the grade levels. Supplementary guidance in the teacher's helps suggests exactly where in lesson plans these may fit in. Teaching pictures, charts, work diagrams, posters, records or soundsheets, filmstrips, and other items can bring variety and a useful multiple-sensory approach to teaching.

Some advantages

1. Audio-visuals can lend variety and appeal to classroom through senses some students can utilize better than through reading and discussion.

2. These aids can provide needed information in ways many learners can more easily remember and utilize than what they can get from printed sources.

3. Audio-visuals open up gates of learning involving all the senses, helping to educate the whole learner in multifaceted ways.

Disadvantages

1. Equipment involved may be difficult to use, cumbersome, and expensive.

2. Content may lull recipients into a merely passive or receptive state and discourage active involvement.

3. The novelty of presentation may overshadow ideas being dealt with.

4. Audio-visuals may crowd out time needed for direct involvement of learners and application of session points to life.

Learning Centers

Recent years have seen the emergence and rapid spread of learning centers through American classrooms. In this approach a number of areas are established in or around a classroom where students may pursue a variety of learning activities at their own pace. The teacher's role becomes one of planning and setting up these centers, perhaps with the help of the learners themselves, and of standing by to assist learners who have questions and other concerns.

An example of the kind of setup that could be made might be a classroom in which a collection of books is arranged in one corner. A reading assignment poster explains to learners just what readings they may do and what questions their reading will answer. In another part of the room, students may listen to teaching records. In a third area they work on creating posters illustrating a certain point. In another center they work at filling in details on a large map of the path of Paul's missionary journeys. In another center two or three children may play a Bible game together. Everything there is designed to help fulfill specific learning goals for a session or unit in a curriculum plan.

A learning center may be carried out on any age level. A given setup may serve for several sessions and then be changed. It may be available just at the normal class period or it may be open at certain hours throughout the week. It is designed to place considerable responsibility on the learner to carry out individual learning activities, to encourage some of the best aspects of the open classroom. It is an extension of the interest or activity centers commonly used with preschool children—their familiar housekeeping center, picture-browsing area, toy center, and the like.

Some advantages

1. The centers encourage learners to be active in their own learning.

2. The centers allow learners to proceed generally at their own best pace for learning.

3. The centers allow to some extent for varying interests and other differences in individual learners.

Some disadvantages

1. The center approach is more elaborate and time-consuming than many teachers are willing to undertake regularly.

2. The unmotivated learner may have difficulty in sticking with learning center approaches over a period of time.

3. Many (but certainly not all) learning center activities lean on individual learning approaches to the extent that they lose the values of peer group learning.

Classroom Worship

This phase of many class sessions is often not understood as a learning activity in itself. It may be seen simply as a routine to be accomplished or an independent but worthy experience having little to do with the rest of what happens in class. Actually classroom worship can be significant as a learning activity even while it serves to bring the learner and God into active communication. In fact, classroom worship may be one of the most distinctive learning activities related to Christian education. While the Holy Spirit is at work in the classroom in many ways—in more ways than we dream of—the approaches here in worship may open the door to student awareness in this realm.

All of the learning tasks may be fostered or heightened through classroom worship. Listening and responding to the gospel is a central function of the worship periods. Because of this learning function it is well if aspects of worship—prayer together, singing, reading the Bible in a worshipful and meditative way and not always simply for "study," and other meditation times—be employed as an integral part of the class session. This means worship would not always be isolated from the rest of the session in some sort of miniature church service.

It is sometimes appropriate to employ worship near the beginning of the class. Here we invite God to join in our exploration and to guide us into all truth. It may come near the end of the session, perhaps as an act of commitment to the things we have been studying about and the right choices that have opened up to us. It could come in the middle as we seek the Spirit's help in making right choices from among alternatives being developed, as we seek new insight into the Bible passage under consideration.

Some advantages

1. Classroom worship helps us draw in a deliberate way on the presence of the Holy Spirit in our learning process.

2. Classroom worship well done can guide students into a God-awareness that they can employ in their lives through the week.

3. Classroom worship can be effective in bringing a felt awareness of God into the classroom and into the learning that should be taking place there.

Some disadvantages

1. Classroom worship can quickly become trite and routine unless carefully planned and sensitively led.

2. Learner moods may not always and automatically be ready for this, and it can be less than meaningful to students in such instances; in fact, it can even turn sometimes into a negative factor.

Printed Resources for Learners

Normally, considerable time is spent in a class session with the student resource as provided in the church curriculum. Most of the time that resource is intended chiefly for the class session rather than for advance study of a lesson. Generally, printed guidance will suggest just how the resources are to be used. The teacher will want to be especially sure that the material is used across the quarter in a variety of ways and that it does not remain always a central item to which the students are required to turn constantly in slavish fashion.

In general the student piece will supply activities to be carried out, pictures to look at, questions to be answered, stories and other items to be read and reported on, skits to be acted out, songs to be sung, facts and other content to be read and reacted to. The teacher will certainly wish to avoid simply taking turns reading in the student piece or reading large sections of it in class as the teacher. The teacher will want to avoid steady use of this material in one routine way. Sometimes he or she may even want to cut apart the resource materials and bring them out as individual items.

Some advantages

1. The printed resources provide consistent, convenient classroom tools.

2. The student pieces generally will provide a helpful variety of classroom procedures.

3. The student pieces readily provide facts and other materials for student learning.

Some disadvantages

1. The student piece may provide a crutch for the class that cuts down on the variety of activities used in the session.

2. The student piece may become so routine and be so narrowly used that students grow bored with the resources and even rebel against them.

Lecture

This is actually a rather broad term for presentations by the teacher. It involves presentations, usually short, in which needed information and issues are brought into the classroom. Generally, the lecture step in a class session would be no more than five or ten minutes long. Often it would be illustrated by charts, pictures, or diagrams. Sometimes it would be laced with humor. It should come in such an informal atmosphere most of the time that students would feel free to react with meaningful questions and comments. Lecture times need to be carefully prepared and done with a lot of eye contact between teachers and learners.

The lecture can be a highly efficient way for learning to take place among well-motivated students and when a central purpose of that part of a class session is to provided needed information. They should not be the central activity in most sessions. They should be extremely well prepared and carried out in a relaxed atmosphere. It is sometimes helpful to introduce a brief lecture by giving learners some things to watch for, some questions that they will be asked to discuss growing out of the lecture.

Lectures can be modified for variety's sake to take on aspects of the interview approach, through role playing by the lecturer, by demonstrations, and in many other ways. Avoid reading lecture material or doing it in a hum-drum kind of way. Recognize that some teachers are going to be better at this than others and that if not skillfully done it should be avoided.

Some advantages

1. Lecture can be a highly efficient way of sharing information among motivated learners.

2. Lecture covers a great deal of material rapidly under strong control by the teacher.

3. Lecture fits in well with the learning preferences of at least some students and is nonthreatening.

Some disadvantages

1. Lecture is easily disappointing and ineffective when not well done.

2. Most students have learning preferences and abilities that make more active learning styles most acceptable.

3. Lecture may contribute to making the Sunday school class boring and a weak imitation of the sermon in the morning worship service.

TEACHING ON THE AGE LEVELS

Notes to Teachers of Young Children

Using the list of criteria for teaching activities in this chapter and your knowledge of young children, check out the suitability of the following storytelling activity for three- and four-year-olds.

Mrs. Jones called together the eight children from her class for storytime. She sat on the carpet with them in the circle around her. The associate teacher, Mr. Keller, sat in the circle opposite her. She proceeded to tell the story of David and his friendship with Jonathan, pointing now and then to a picture of the two. Once in a while, she would ask the children to help her by mentioning a word she needed to round out the story. When three-year-old Adam's attention wavered at one point, Mr. Keller noted that and helped draw him back into the situation with a special comment that Adam responded to.

At the end of the story, Mrs. Jones said, "We are good friends, too, aren't we? How can we be like David and Jonathan that way?" Mr. Keller drew a picture of a boy helping a girl who was crying because she had bumped her head on the table.

In telling the story, Mrs. Jones was very animated. She smiled and twice she hugged the children near her to show her own friendly spirit. She knew the story well by heart and maintained good eye contact with each of the children. She also showed the children in the big classroom Bible where this story was to be found. She kept close to the Bible account but filled in some imaginative details as she told the story.

Studying this chapter in light of early childhood: Consider the place of storytelling in teaching young children. What do you learn from the description of Mrs. Jones' storytelling? As carried out here, how would this activity test according to the list of criteria for appropriate teaching activities? If you were coaching other teachers of children in storytelling, what would you emphasize for them? Also, prepare a list of other teaching activities that seem basic and important for teaching young children.

Notes to Teachers of Elementary Children

Check out the suitability of this activity as described for elementary children.

Dick George wanted to help children in his class know and understand the Great Commission, Matthew 28:19: "Therefore go and make disciples." So he placed a large blank sheet of paper on the table around which his class sometimes sat. He described the setting in which Jesus gave this commission to his followers. Then he asked the girls and boys to look up the verse in their Bibles. They found the passage and they took turns writing the verse in large letters on the paper.

When it was completed they tacked the verse up on the bulletin

107

board and repeated it together several times in unison. Then Mr. George asked them if they could repeat it together when he took the sheet down. After doing this two times he asked for volunteers to repeat the verse. Two students volunteered and recited it perfectly.Now Mr. George asked the class if they could put the poster back together if they cut the words apart and mixed them all up. The class accepted the challenge and had no trouble putting the verse back together again, with only one small discussion.

"Now, I wonder what some of these words really mean?" Naming three class members, he asked, "Will you three write what you think this word means? There are some dictionaries on the shelf."

Mr. George was using a variety of approaches to memorizing without resorting to the routine. The children came at the verse in a variety of ways: (1) looking it up in their Bibles; (2) placing the verse in a meaningful context; (3) writing the verse out; (4) repeating the verse in unison; (5) individuals repeating the verse and others listening; (6) putting random words of the verse together; (7) discussing the meaning of words in the verse. By the time all of these things had been done, the repetition had built up and the children could repeat the verse with some sense of its meaning.

Studying this chapter in light of elementary childhood: Consider the place of memorizing and related activities in the teaching of elementary children. How do various approaches to memorizing seem to work with children of these ages? How would Mr. George's approaches here test out according to the list of criteria for appropriate teaching activities that appears in this chapter? If you were coaching other teachers in the use of memorization, repetition, reading, and related basic approaches to learning, what would you emphasize? Prepare a list of other teaching activities that you consider basic and important for teaching elementary children.

Note to Teachers of Youth

Check out the suitability of these valuing exercises as appropriate learning activities for youth:

Karen and Mark teach the high school class at their church.

They wish to place considerable emphasis on the youths' attempts to work out their own beliefs and life commitments and not just blindly copy from parents and friends. They are concerned that students choose, clarify, and act on what is important to them. In one class session Karen and Mark were dealing with lifework as a Christian vocation and the call of God to serve him in daily work.

"Now as you think about what you might do in your life work, we want you to compare some possibilities and take your stand along the line we have put down," Mark said. He pointed to a ribbon of masking tape the couple had pasted down on the floor running fifteen feet through the middle of the classroom. At one end they placed a sign: "Well-paying job with much security." At the other end was a sign: "Job that serves other people, provides personal satisfaction, but is low paying."

The students then took up a position along the line, many clustering near the middle. Karen asked this group, "Why are you standing there? Are you afraid to make a choice between one or the other? Or are you looking for both?" This started a discussion that caused some of the youth to move toward one end of the line or the other, and some others at the ends moved as well. They were taking a public stand along a continuum regarding the values they have for their lifework.

As the students continued to stand along the line, Karen and Mark interviewed each one about the reasons for taking the position they have. They were called upon to make a public statement of their convictions. Some strengthened their views. Others changed their minds as the conversation proceeded. This involved a couple of activities sometimes associated with values formation. On an issue that really has several aspects, the teachers asked their students to make a free choice, carefully thought out, something they were ready to commit to. Then they had to take a public stand for what they believe, reflect on it, and be able to state why they chose as they did.

A range of related activities are commonly employed in helping young people and adults learn through choice making, reflection, and commitment responses.

Studying this chapter in light of youth: Consider the place of valuing activities in the teaching of youth. How do various approaches to choice making and commitment fit in with adolescent readiness and interests? How well do these activities in your experience or in your opinion, work out in youth classes generally? How would Karen and Mark's particular approach here test out according to the list of criteria for appropriate teaching activities in this chapter? If you were coaching other teachers on the use of valuing activities for youth, what would you emphasize? Prepare a list of other basic teaching activities that you consider important in the teaching of young persons.

Notes to Teachers of Adults

The Pathfinders Bible Class was known as a group who really enjoyed a good discussion. Some of the credit for that would go to their teacher, Harvey Jackson. It was said he really knew how to spark a discussion, keep it going, and help the class get somewhere with it.

One Sunday the Pathfinders were having a session on forgiveness and reconciliation based on Joseph's treatment of his brothers. After reviewing the story with his class Mr. Jackson asked them to list some signs of spiritual maturity in Joseph. He asked the class to think privately about some of the things that other people have done that hurt them most.

Then he posed this question for discussion: "What are some of the things that make it hard to forgive?" Later he would ask: "How do we overcome these barriers to offering forgiveness?"

In the process of discussion, Mr. Jackson was careful not to express his own opinions on the question early. He welcomed all contributions, making sure that reasonable accuracy was maintained in any data used and doing that without embarrassing anyone. Where comments were not heard by everyone he repeated them. He occasionally summed up where the class was in its discussion.

The class itself, composed of about twenty-five persons, was seated informally in a two-row semicircle. After seven or eight minutes on each of the two main questions, he summed up and moved on to a concluding phase of the session. Mr. Jackson made sure he had clear, discussible questions where a range of possibilities could be brought into the situation. He worked to avoid pat "Sunday school" answers. He marked progress and tried to help everyone feel comfortable. He made sure the discussion grew out of some data that the class had generally shared and would not just be a matter of personal prejudice or uninformed assumptions.

Studying this chapter in light of adulthood: Consider the place of discussion activities in teaching adults. How do the various approaches to discussion—small group work, partner nudging, lecture and response, question and answer, dialogue, and the like—fit in with adult readiness, needs, and background? How well does genuine discussion of issues work out generally in adult classes you know?

How would Harvey Jackson's approach here test out according to the list of criteria for appropriate teaching activities? If you were coaching other teachers of adults on the use of discussion activities, what would you emphasize? Prepare a list of other basic teaching activities that you consider important in the teaching of adults.

STUDYING THIS CHAPTER IN CLASS

Possible Goals
    • To develop guidelines for selecting and using the most mean ingful teaching methods.

    • To survey some basic teaching methods, consider how to use them, and understand their advantages and disadvantages.

A Class Plan
    1. Introduce the session by explaining that teachers are always using some method or activity to help people learn. Methods and how we use them are important.

    2. Survey some typical learning situations. (Ask class members to share memories of how they have spent most of the time in

classes they recall from church or school. Some may remember long lectures, painful lesson recitals, good times working on projects, helpful discussions, and other procedures. Fill in their remembrances with some of the instances listed under the section "Some Learning Situations" from this chapter.)

3. Brainstorm a list of learning activities. (Ask one member of the class to record the ideas of the class on chalkboard or large sheets of paper. Ask the class members to make a list of as many teaching methods or activities as they can come up with in a set time period of five or ten minutes. See how long a list you can get without stopping now to evaluate. Allow hitchhiking to develop further some previous ideas.)

4. Build a list of criteria for judging the suitability of given teaching methods. (This can emerge through class discussion based on the material found following Checklist for Learning Activities, pages 90–95.)

5. Discuss how to conduct certain basic teaching methods of particular interest to those in the class, noting advantages and disadvantages. (Refer to the brainstorming list evolved by the students and ask which one or two they would like to see discussed further. If the class is large and you have resource persons, it could divide into interest groups by age levels or by such basic methods as discussion, storytelling, or valuing exercises.)

6. Where possible let students plan and carry out a basic teaching method in a Sunday school class or in the group studying this course together.

I planted the seed, Apollos watered it, but God made it grow. So neither he who plants nor he who waters is anything, but only God, who makes things grow…. For we are God's fellow workers; you are God's field, God's building.

—1 Corinthians 3:6–9, NIV

Chapter 6

Bridges to Class Preparation

- *Where in the world do I start in order to teach a lesson?*
- *Do I have to use the curriculum plan as it appears inprint?*
- *Is it every teacher for himself/herself or are we part of a team?*
- *I hate to evaluate things after I've done them. Do I need to?*

When it comes to planning, the world is full of all kinds of people. Some like for things to be spontaneous and just happen. Others must plan very carefully and in great detail. Some plan far ahead, and others live close to deadlines. Good teaching calls for some of all of this. It is good to plan carefully ahead and to live and work by some great, overarching plans. But it is also good to be open and flexible to what comes up at the moment. The Holy Spirit can work with us through all those situations. Since we do come in all kinds of shapes and sizes, let's meet more closely some of these varied planning types:

Rigid Robert: He likes to plan everything down to the last detail and well in advance. He finds security in having it that way; it takes the worry out of the job, he says. He firmly believes in the importance of careful planning, both in his work and in his service in the church. At the same time he feels uncomfortable if his careful plan is interrupted or threatened by anything. He attempts to stay exactly on plan right down to the minute across an entire curriculum unit. He won't discuss anything "off the subject" that students bring up or adjust to meet emerging situations.

Flexible Felix: He's flexible to the point of wanting almost no plan at all. He likes to deal with emerging needs and concerns that pop up. So he prepares only in the most general kind of way and relies on his broad knowledge and the leading of the moment. He would be disappointed, in fact, if his little plan went through without change. He figures the students would not be interested.

Deadline Dana: She figures that she does her best when she is under pressure. Therefore, she doesn't do anything about preparing her session until the very last minute, Saturday evening at the earliest, and sometimes on her way to church. She comes up with some good things in the process, but usually she is limited to the most simple directions provided in her teacher's guide. She wouldn't begin to think about a whole unit of lessons at a time or the long-range flow of the curriculum. It's a matter of just barely beating the deadline.

Isolated Isabel: Isabel operates primarily in the here and now. She wants to focus strongly on the particular children she is teaching this Sunday with their needs and interests as they are right now. She doesn't want to be burdened or have her focus blunted by trying to keep in mind a lot of other things—like what other classes are studying, the church year, the long-term curriculum plan, and the like. "It's just those kids and me dealing with the gospel," she has sometimes said.

There are obvious advantages and some disadvantages in each of these approaches. Without good planning, carefully but flexibly followed, we are going to face some difficulty. Without fitting ourselves flexibly and with spontaneity into a larger picture, we are going to limit our ministry. Balance in creating and carrying out a session plan within a larger unit and within a larger curriculum plan is the key.

Part of a Big Plan

Sunday school teachers can multiply the effectiveness of their teaching and understand in a far better way how to make a contribution to the overall education of their students if they can teach from within a larger plan. That means knowing, understanding, and teaching within a broad educational or curricular plan to which their church is committed. It means identifying where their students are on the learner track, what their past experience has been, and where they are going. In this way, teachers don't teach for this Sunday and the next in isolation but as a part of a larger system to which they can make a careful contribution.

A typical curriculum plan focuses its activities in the direction of one general purpose for the church it its educational mission. Purpose or mission statements often seek in a unified way to stress the centrality of Christ and his redeeming love, the faith responses of persons, and the basis of the entire approach in the Bible. They tend to see the church's educational work as a ministry that is part of the whole ministry of the church involving whole persons. Many church groups and curriculum plans have such central statements available. It is a useful exercise for local congregations to develop thoughtfully their own purpose or mission statements by which to guide their ministry.

Local educational ministry should keep such a statement in mind as a focal point as the church engages in such varied settings as child care, youth ministry, or adult Bible study. The mission or purpose statement anchors the general curriculum plan. One such statement for curriculum materials is this: "The mission of the Sunday school curriculum is to provide resources for the systematic study of the Bible with an awareness of our Christian heritage and for the application of biblical truth to life today."

A number of curriculum plans provide a track that will take the learner through a three-year cycle with a different common theme being followed each three months. In *Bridges* curriculum, for example, quarterly perspectives begin in the fall with Revelation and move through Redemption in the winter, Church or Community in the spring, and Discipleship in the summer.

On each age level come study units appropriate for that age level but with some common ties through the quarterly themes and the Uniform Lesson units. These units break down into weekly sessions. Or they may be seen as projects or modules of experience that the class will undertake as it makes its way through the unit. These units and sessions each have goal or objective statements. Biblical passages and special emphases have been assigned by the planners of the resources to make distinctive emphases each session and at the same time build on each other toward unit goals.

On occasion, usually about once a quarter, it is appropriate for all age levels to be studying the same general Bible passage although from their own perspectives. This is known as an Anchor Sunday. Here the morning worship service and the sermon can sometimes be tied in as well.

Typical curriculum plans following a group-graded approach would provide a range of materials for early childhood, some for families of infants, some for children ages two and three. Kindergarten material is designed generally to serve ages four and five. Early Elementary material is planned for grades 1 and 2 (the child just learning to read). Middle Elementary material is planned for grades 3 and 4. Some flexibility is possible in all of this. Upper Elementary material is planned for grades 5 and 6 with some linkages to Younger Youth, which provides for grades 7 and 8 (and possibly grades 6 or 9 depending on the local school situation). Older Youth serves the young person of high school age.

Adult curriculum serves generally, with teacher and class adaptations, across the total adult span. Here grouping and grading take a variety of forms. Perhaps the most common one is for an adult class to be formed by young adults with common family and career interests on a short-term basis.

Smaller congregations often have simply a class of younger adults and another of older adults. Some churches are able to minister to special needs through classes for singles, young converts, young parents, and other specialized concerns. A range of elective courses may be offered across these age levels within the general curriculum plan. Blessed are those teachers who know that their teaching fits into a bigger picture, that they have a special contribution to make to build up the whole, and that they don't have to do it all this Sunday or next. They see themselves as teaching in a big system that bridges to what happens within the family, in the general church services, and in special ministries among children, youth, and adults.

Teach with a Purpose

In describing this larger educational plan of which each class can be a part, we have already encountered the idea of objectives and purposes. An educational ministry takes on unity and overall shape when it has one central objective. This can be expressed through objectives, aims, or goals for units and sessions.

Objectives, especially for a unit or session, can be more helpful to us than most of us let them be. We can use them to judge what goes into a unit or a session and what stays out. They can help us see how sessions build through a unit and how each is distinct from the other. They can build to help ensure a bridging between the learner's immediate concerns and the main emphases of the gospel. They can sometimes point in open-ended fashion toward high challenges and allow for whatever student growth may come about. Or they set up such specific goals that the student and the class will clearly understand when they have accomplished them.

Let's examine some different types of objective/goal statements and see what they say, don't say, and how they can serve us. Here are some examples:

"To consider how our failures and discouragements in Christian living can become stepping-stones to further growth as children of God."

This objective is addressed to the entire class as a learning community, both teachers and students, and assumes they will be exploring and learning together. It is open-ended in that it does not list some specifics that the class will either clearly accomplish or fail to accomplish. The objective takes in current life situations—failures and discouragements. It also points vertically to God through its reference to living that is Christian and to our relationships as God's children.

"To help students discover how their failures and discouragements in Christian living can become stepping-stones to further growth as children of God." This objective differs from the previous one in that it is directed to the teacher and suggests that the teacher's goal is to help students explore. Here the attention is not on the learning community of teacher and student together, but on a teacher who is going to try to cause certain things to happen in the class. The teacher in this learning scheme is seen as a separate person from the students. The teacher's learning along with the students' is not considered here. This is known as an instrumental purpose.

"To write out three ways of dealing with failure and success in Christian living and to practice using those ways in class." This goal statement is a behavioral goal in that it specifically describes behavior or activities that the class will go through. The teacher will then know exactly when that objective has been fulfilled. When this goal is accomplished the teacher will not really know if the students are growing as Christians. But the teacher will know if the class has carried out certain activities, fed back certain teachings. The class will go through certain prescribed procedures. Something measurable will have been carried out.

Often teachers can develop their own very specific objectives that can measure their progress and apply specifically to their class from the more general goal statement supplied in resources. Those who prepare general resources for use widely across the country cannot know all the very specific and definite needs of learners in a given class. A session can come to a much stronger focus if it can center on a precise and specific goal drawn to fit the needs of the class. Taking inventory of those needs in relation to the session as suggested by the curriculum plan enables a teacher to come up with a relevant purpose. A session plan should start with and each step or part of it should be governed by how it contributes to some fulfillment of the plan.

Occasionally a range of goals may be suggested, with class members choosing those they wish to use. The important point is ultimately to focus on controlling goals that give central focus to what we undertake and help us measure how we are doing.

Planning a Session

The typical class session plan has a beginning, a step-by-step development, and a conclusion. This is the usual kind of session for which teaching resources give guidance in more or less detail. We shall explore other ways of structuring a class session.

Leading into the Session

In drawing up a class plan, you need to plan carefully how you will begin. That beginning generally will take place as soon as the first student arrives. You will be thinking about how you will be relating to that person, what kind of conversation you will have, what activity you might have available for that person to enter into immediately. Then as soon as most of the class members have arrived, what will you all be doing together? The beginning is important. It must capture the students' attention if you are ever really going to have it during the session. The beginning should set the pace for the whole class period. It should honestly indicate something of what the session is going to be all about. It should open up a mood of exploring and discovering and build a sense of expectation about what is going to happen later in the period.

Leading through the Session

The steps that come next should follow a logical development and take the students through some variety of teaching activities, some change of pace and style and mood. Younger learners, at least (older ones, too?), need some opportunity to get up and move around. Youth classes may well move, for instance, from a learning game to a discussion to a skit and back to discussion, rather than follow a whole-class discussion pattern throughout.

Leading beyond the Session

The conclusion should be as carefully planned as anything else. Sometimes it will summarize and wrap up things. But not always. There is value at times in leaving loose ends dangling, in not neatly tying everything together at the end of the session. That may allow students to continue to wrestle with ideas, to keep on thinking about the session, to work things through on their own. Of course, when you do this, you will want to be careful to get back the next week or with each student to work things through and to handle any problems that students may be having with what was discussed. Often the conclusion is related to the learning task of taking personal responsibility in a given area. Projects may be decided on. Follow-up and continuing activities may be discussed. Commitments may be made in a matter-of-fact or very worshipful way.

Types of Session Development

These step-by-step session plans generally follow one of three main flows from a logical standpoint. They may begin with a proposition, an affirmation, a matter of faith from which the class draws meaning for life. This is the kind of approach where the class might start by studying a Bible passage. From it they draw meaning for life. This is approach is sometimes diagrammed as follows:

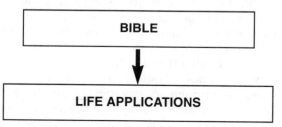

This is a pattern that is most easily recognized as a strongly Bible-centered or Bible-focused session. Very often the units in this approach are structured as studies of books of the Bible or of great biblical themes.

Another basic approach is to follow some principle such as, "Begin where the students are." Here we open with life situations, concerns, or problems. These are thoroughly examined. Then we turn to the resources the church has to offer, most commonly the

Bible and a passage listed for the session in order to find help in dealing with the problems identified. This approach is sometimes diagrammed this way:

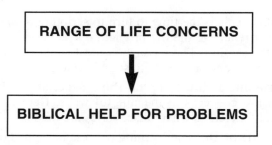

This approach is often regarded as a life-centered or person-focused approach. Here units and sessions are frequently structured around areas of student need, and this is the most obvious feature of them. Yet this approach can also be very biblical.

A third approach is an extension of the method just described. Here we start off with life concerns, turn to a Bible passage for possible help, and then draw from the passage its chief meanings and applications. This places the Bible material central in the session, with part of the session moving toward it and part of the session drawing from it:

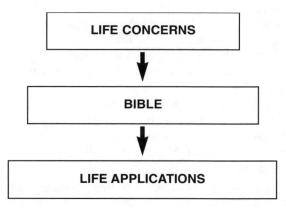

A typical session flow is known as the ABCD approach:

A—Awareness. This is the opening, usually designed to capture the learner's attention and to relate to them where they have life concerns.

B—Bible. This is the time to turn to scripture to explore a Bible passage that relates to the life problem opened up in the Awareness phase of the session. The passage is most soundly offered when it is set in context and studied with sound principles of interpretation.

C—Crossing Point. Here the Bible material just interpreted is related to life concerns in meaningful ways. Here is where Bible bridges to life. Here is where discoveries are made.

D—Decide or Do. The learning process is capped off by important life decisions made in light of biblical teaching and by actions that put those teachings into practice.

The end result of any of these approaches can be that the Bible is brought into meaningful relationship with life problems, and crossing points are set up. There are those who feel that for a study to be fully biblical, it needs to be structured by the Bible and begin with a study of a Bible passage. But if the Bible passage is turned to as a help in meeting a problem, that can be just as soundly biblical if the passage is studied with integrity and if good principles of interpretation are used.

What may happen, of course, is that a class may never move far from where it begins. If it begins with the Bible and never really gets to life meanings, then bridges between Bible and life have not been set up. If the class begins with life and never moves beyond the surveying of human problems to any kind of light from the Bible, once again a crossing point has not been structured and the whole is weakened.

We don't have to be wed to any one of these approaches alone. As a matter of fact, the class may be more interesting and therefore of more value to the students if these basic approaches vary from week to week or unit to unit. Variety, carefully injected, can be the spice of a class's life.

Each step in a teaching plan needs to be a wedding of two basic elements. One is a clear concept to be worked on, a concept that falls within the scope of the session as defined by its purpose statement. The other element is the activity, method, or process of teaching that is to be followed in order for that concept to be explored. We really don't have a session step until we have a clear idea of both concept and activity, fitting smoothly together.

So a step-by-step session plan in its essential elements includes these elements: (1) a specific session goal that controls each teaching step we take; (2) a way of beginning that involves students as they arrive and the entire group, something striking and interesting to them; (3) a series of clear-cut session steps (two to five) listing both a concept to be taught and a way of teaching it; and (4) a conclusion that wraps up the session or intentionally leaves it open for further exploration.

Where discussion is the backbone of the plan, the basic discussion questions should be listed as part of the session steps. The plan should provide for strong student involvement. It should call for some change of pace in activity as we move through the session. It should provide needed information and lead to some desired change by the learners. Last, it should focus clearly on biblical concepts, using sound interpretation.

The plan should be dedicated to flexible execution. Overriding student concerns may come up. Fruitful areas of exploration we have not anticipated may grow out of earlier stages of the session. Student response may go in unanticipated ways. And so the door toward flexibility always needs to be kept open, without the teacher giving in to mere delaying tactics or game playing by students intent on seeing how disruptive they can be.

Not every class session plan need follow this step-by-step approach. Elsewhere we have discussed the learning center. Here various learning activities for individuals and small groups are set up by areas in a room. Students move from one to the next usually at their own pace throughout the session.

A unit may center around a project or group of projects. The class begins by planning out its projects together and then working on them, often by small teams across several weeks. The unit culminates when the project is put on display or put into action. Each session is simply a work period. It involves research in the Bible and elsewhere, planning things out, working on the props, talking about it, evaluating what is being done. Each session of this type does not stand alone. It is not centered in the teacher, and it is not carried out according to a common pattern of steps.

Other approaches may be used to teach a unit as a whole across a period of weeks rather than in separate session chunks. One week the class members may plan for a play. The next week they may present the play before their parents or other interested people. The third week they may discuss what happened and what the play taught. This and other approaches may vary widely from traditional step-by-step session plans and can bring enriching variety to many classes.

Use of the Bible

Let it be understood that curriculum plans can make several different kinds of use of the Bible that are equally valid. Currently the church makes of the Sunday church school a system for basic teaching and understands the Bible as its principal communicator of God's authoritative word and our chief guide for faith and action. That being true, the Bible will continue to need central consideration in the teaching-learning process. That attention needs to be more than paying the Bible reverence, and it needs to be something different from a kind of worship of the Bible for its own sake, a mere bibliolatry.

Normally teachers have seen their main use of the Bible with children as the telling of Bible stories. Educators disagree about the effectiveness and suitability of using a great many Bible stories with young children. Some feel that heavy, repeated use of a few basic and most universally understood Bible stories such as the good Samaritan and the prodigal son will mean that by the time the learner has grown mature enough for full understanding of those stories they will have grown threadbare in the telling. They may seem so old and dull that the learner is no longer open to finding new and fuller meaning in them.

Some people feel that many stories just aren't suitable for young children because of the behavior of characters, the violence, or the difficult concepts. Some would admit these things but would still

124

see value in telling the stories to young children as a part of their Christian heritage. Girls and boys can know and appreciate some stories as a part of their background and as a part of the Christian faith even though they may not yet fully understand them. A middle ground here would suggest a broad use of Bible stories with kindergarten children, for instance, while avoiding the more complex and violent ones. This can be done without the need for children to grasp the full meaning of the story.

At the same time it is good to keep in mind that while God's story is central in the Bible, it is more than a book of stories. Many other concepts that are taught in the Bible need to be introduced to children. It is valid to do this not only through direct reference to the Bible, but also through illustrating those concepts by stories from our own day and other teaching devices. To do so is biblical, too.

When using the Bible with older children, the simpler language of many present-day translations can be helpful. Avoid confusing young children with a variety of translations. It is well to use those translations considered most accurate and to avoid frequent use of the translations that claim only to be paraphrases.

Studying passages in their context is a serious requirement. While there is room for tracing some of the great themes of the Bible by passages found here and there throughout the Scriptures, most approaches to the Bible should avoid use of proof texts—coming up with verses from here and there selected especially to support some argument or point the teacher wants to make. Instead, passages should be chosen that include the entire event involved, that hang together as a unit. They should be studied with an eye to what kind of literature this is, who was writing to whom, and why. This kind of information can often be found in the teacher's helps and in standard reference books such as Bible dictionaries, commentaries, and study Bibles.

In looking at the passage itself a variety of methods and approaches can add significance to our work. Paraphrasing of verses following study of the real meaning of the passage, translating the passage into skit form, making pictures that illustrate the meaning, writing commentaries, answering questions, memorizing, telling a friend the meaning in your own words, comparing translations—these are but a few of dozens of categories of activities that may bring richness to our study of the Scriptures.

Assignments and Projects

What should be expected of the student outside of class? Should the student "study a lesson" in advance? What other kinds of relationship outside the classroom should the teacher seek to build among students?

The classroom time is so limited that the more ways the teacher finds to extend contacts beyond the usual forty minutes to an hour on Sunday morning the more effective the teacher can be. But routine expectations that students will study their lessons in advance and come to class prepared to discuss them are usually doomed to failure, especially in youth and elementary classes. The frustration is built in. Suppose a few conscientious students do prepare. Do we assume that all students have prepared and go from there? That will lose the majority who have not studied. Or do we get practical and assume that most students have not prepared? That leaves those who have worked ahead being overprepared, their advance study having apparently been done in vain. Or if we draw on the prepared ones and lecture those who have not, we start off on a bad footing with many students.

The answer does not seem to be routine lesson study by all the students. There is more to be gained by making special assignments. Find out the individual skills of your students and build on those as you individualize the things you ask students to do to help you carry out the session. Students can use their hobbies—photography, for instance—to help prepare a special report in advance. Or they can record an interview on a tape cassette or come ready to act out a skit. Assignments tailored to the special skills and interests of students can pay off.

Other projects can grow out of class sessions. In order to put feet on the gospel the students may agree to help an elderly woman who lives alone clean up her yard and house. They work on that together in the week following class. Or, the class members may decide on a field trip. They will visit a special display of religious art at a museum or visit the county home. At other levels class members may find themselves together for other activities during the week on a regular basis.

Beyond class meetings and projects, the teacher will seek to know the students in their homes and to get acquainted with their parents. Regular plans for visitation are important. We will be on the phone frequently with students, certainly not just to check up on absences and illnesses but as friend to friend: "Just thought I'd give you a ring and see how things are going this week." Where homes and teachers have access to fax and E-mail, that can bring interesting variety to these contacts. Ties that reach across the week will pay off in good relationships on Sunday morning, in better discipline, in effective learning.

Evaluation

The teaching of a session or unit is not complete until it has been evaluated. At least brief informal moments of looking back at what has happened in a class session are valuable even for the youngest classes. Beyond that, the teacher will always be thinking about what happened in a session or unit and considering its value. What worked? What didn't work? Why was there this measure of success or failure? What needs to be changed when this is done the next time? What were the students' responses? Are there signs that they learned some things in the direction of our purposes? Think about the learners individually as much as possible. What needs and concerns did they bring to the sessions? How were these dealt with? What new or persistent needs emerged and are now clearly before us? What were our feelings as teachers? Were we comfortable at some points, uncomfortable at others?

With answers to such questions in mind, we begin to think how to apply all of this to our next teaching assignment.

Evaluation doesn't call for any special talent, but practice and experience help us get the most out of it. It is an essential element in the ongoing cycle of teaching.

Thoughtful and careful teachers will find themselves evaluating and learning much from this process for more effective work in God's kingdom as the future unfolds. Thinking back and planning ahead are important ways for us to build bridges of effective teaching.

TEACHING ON AGE LEVELS

Notes to Teachers of Young Children

Here are some suggestions for planning learning sessions for young children. Please react to or expand on these.

A. Keep short attention spans in mind. Plan to change the pace and the style of the learning session often during the period. The child's span of attention is lengthening across these years, but do not depend on a child continuing to do one thing over extended time. Stories need to be fairly short. Allow for movement from one interest to another. Expect the patterns of play to change rapidly.

B. Build around activity. Don't demand too much quiet sitting by most children of this age. Some exceptions will quickly come to mind, but as a group the children need to be on the go and moving frequently during the period. Give them things to do. Stand by to help it all stay on the orderly side, but expect things to be full of life.

C. Make it friendly and informal. Demonstrate the kind of behavior that will help the young child decide that church is a happy place to be. Avoid too much sitting around in stiff rows or even a perfect circle. Avoid expecting everything to happen at a table. It is good if you can have a carpeted floor, bright, sunny, well-lit rooms, and a variety of toys and other equipment to provide for active children.

D. Expect and plan play. Since play is the children's principal "work" and avenue of learning, count on them to make play of many things that happen around the class. The teacher's job is often to suggest ways and means of playing and to stand by and deal with the life problems and situations that come up. Often the teacher can help the child reflect on the meanings that come from play.

Studying this chapter in light of early childhood: Start from scratch or use existing study material to make up your very own plan for a learning session with young children. Tie it in with a general purpose for educational ministry and create your own session goal or goals. Decide on how you will have your room arranged and what activities you will have the children engage in. Make a general plan providing change of pace, a variety of activities, and other essentials in a teaching-learning session for young children. Discuss your plan with other teachers.

Notes to Teachers of Elementary Children

In its best sense, discipline is more related to learning than it is to enforced good behavior. Teachers of elementary children, sometimes beset by what they call discipline problems, can avoid some of those by following good disciplinary principles in their session planning and in carrying those plans out with a sense of understanding, good cheer, fairness, and realistic expectations of their children. Here are some discipline suggestions for you to react to or expand upon:

A. Be interesting. That doesn't need to turn you into an entertainer, but it does caution against boring children. Choose a variety of activities for your lesson plan. Build a repertoire of those that you learn by experience will keep the attention of children.

B. Be well prepared. Know exactly what you want to do. Have all the needed materials at hand. Move easily and smoothly from one activity to the next without too much fumbling and wandering. Be purposeful; know where you are going and move along expectantly looking forward with the class to the next step of the session.

C. Relate personally. Foster good, warm, healthy relationships with class members as individuals. Become their friends. Maintain high expectations with a kindly, openhearted spirit. Such ties are likely to encourage the children to want to cooperate and please their good adult friend, the teacher.

D. Don't expect perfect deportment all the time. Be a little flexible in this direction. Children and teachers are both human and sometimes need to break away from the controlling matter of the moment in the class plan. They may need to talk with neighbors.

They may need to complain occasionally. Don't demand to hear a pin drop in a children's class.

Studying this chapter in light of elementary childhood: Develop a class teaching plan for a selected group of elementary children. Originate your own plan or modify existing materials to fit your own needs. Tie it in with a general purpose for educational ministry and create your own session goals. Make a general plan for teaching the session through a series of steps listing specific activities wedded with matter to be taught and suggesting a time frame. Give special consideration concerning how the plan may support in a positive way the discipline of learning. Share your plan with other teachers as you evaluate it together.

Notes to Teachers of Youth

Continuity. In many ways each session plan for youth needs to stand on its own. There may be considerable coming and going among individual youth, and with a week between classes it is good to plan for each session to be a separate and complete experience.

Continuity and building from one session to the next, however, is increasingly possible with youth. They have the capacity to put together concepts studied last week and a month ago to build into something new. It is good for youth classes to take advantage of that. This makes the unit approach, quarterly emphasis, and general goals for youth across a year or so all the more significant.

There is value in the teacher being able to move with flexibility to deal with emerging issues or hot topics that have arisen in the lives of young persons. Allowance should be made for this. Yet, sometimes these can be handled in other youth ministry settings so that a course of study with continuity across an extended period of time can be maintained with some integrity.

Continuity suggests also a whole approach to teaching, often involving a team. It is good for the teachers to be in class steadily, week after week, month after month. Sometimes any necessary absences will not be so obvious if a teaching team works together on coverage. In any case, when a team works together any transitions in leadership during the session should be smooth; both members of the team should be fully active in the process throughout the period even if one is taking the lead and the other acting as support at a given moment.

Materials. Youth sometimes react against printed study materials, associating them with earlier childhood Sunday school routines or weekday school. Some of that reaction may be a problem with the materials themselves, but more often it is a form of response to routine and sameness in the approach. Teachers may deal with this by de-emphasizing the steady or frequent use of quarterlies or study guides. Sometimes sections can be cut out of the student pieces in advance. Curriculum materials like *Bridges* provide reproducible sheets to be used as handouts. Certainly a teacher should not appear to rely heavily, nose in book, on the teacher's material. That can be a barrier between teacher and learner. Good eye contact and a degree of informality should be a keynote in the class.

Youth are increasingly able to relate class study to outside service projects and other activities. The wholeness of youth ministry can be under girded by deliberate linkages between what is studied on Sunday morning and at other times during the week with service projects, recreation periods, and individual contact.

Studying this chapter in light of youth: Develop a class teaching plan for a selected group of youth, originating your own plan or modifying existing materials. Tie the session in with a general purpose for educational ministry and create your own session goals. Make a general plan for teaching the session through a series of steps listing specific activities wedded with matter to be taught and suggesting a time frame. Give special consideration to how continuity and wholeness in youth ministry may be undergirded by the session. Assume also a teaching team and how its members can relate to each other in this particular session to provide maximum enrichment and wholeness to the process. Discuss your plan with other teachers.

Notes to Teachers of Adults
Adults bring rich and varied background resources to their class-

es. All those years since they were in high school have added up to something. Adults also are concerned that what they are studying have some special relevance to their lives. Here are some hints on planning for discussion as a major part of your teaching plan.

A. Plan key discussion questions carefully and with some anticipation of related questions that are likely to emerge. Write out your questions. Check to see they cannot be answered simply yes or no or with a piece of information. If you simply want information sharing or repetition, use other methods. Questions of why and how are more supportive of discussion than questions of who, what, and when.

B. Submit only matters that are genuinely open and discussible. If there is, in your opinion, only one right answer, handle the matter in some other way than discussion. If there is need for information not generally available to the class before answers can be developed, postpone discussion until data is available and resulting issues are apparent. You must risk the class coming out in a different place from you in matters that are genuinely and freely open to discussion.

C. Don't impose your own answers to the discussion questions too easily, quickly, or even strongly. The class has a right to know where you stand eventually and you have a right to try to influence them, but to make that attempt too early in the discussion will only inhibit thought and conversation.

D. Make sure your questions appear important to the class. The issue should be real, related to their lives, certainly not trite, repetitive, obvious, or humdrum. Some issues that appear obscure on the surface are still important to adults. A number of seemingly fine points of Bible interpretation may appear inconsequential, but if you feel they are important enough to come before a group of modern adults in their Sunday school class, they should be communicated with an eye to their significance, interest, and relevance.

E. Anticipate class response to the discussion as much as you can in order to make the most of resources among students in the class and avoid pitfalls some may pose. Know your students. Know how to draw out helpful feedback from those best equipped to help with an issue. Be ready to deal with problem discussers—the endlessly repetitious, the overly prejudiced, those who tend to dominate things, the ones who are usually a little off focus. You may have to reach private understandings outside of class with some problem discussers. You may have to set up special participation rules.

Learn how to accept a wide range of answers without putting participants down even when you find them in error in some comments.

F. Mark progress in the discussion. Help the class make sense of its discussion as it goes along. Point out progress. Occasionally sum up. Help learners avoid wandering in circles or simply pooling ignorance.

G. Be enough removed from the heat of the discussion that you can have good perspective on it. Listen carefully. Draw things together and point directions as you move toward conclusions. Try to wrap things up in an even-handed, honest way. Most of the time there should be a sense of closure as you end a discussion period, but not always.

H. Remember that there are dozens of ways of carrying out the discussion method, of stimulating it, and moving it along. Data can be introduced in a wide variety of ways and then this can be discussed in small groups, by partners sitting side by side, or in a total group setting. Some discussions can be carried out by a panel in front of the larger group.

Discussion may be stimulated by asking learners to write some of their answers first and then share these. Startling statements can be presented for reaction. Try some one-to-one interviews that can expand to include the whole group. The varieties and tools associated with discussion are endless.

Studying this chapter in light of adults: Develop a class teaching plan for a selected adult group. You may originate your plan or modify existing materials to fit your situation. Tie the session in with a general purpose for educational ministry and create your own session goals. Make a general plan for teaching the session through a series of steps listing specific activities wedded with matter to be taught within a time budget. Give special consideration to planning in some detail for discussion, including the wording of key questions and anticipation of specific needs and responses. Consider variations on basic discussion activities. Share your plan and critique it with other teachers.

STUDYING THIS CHAPTER IN CLASS

Possible Goals

- To gain a picture of the larger curriculum plan of which the teacher is a part.
- To understand what goes into a good lesson plan and to create one.
- To learn how to create and make good use of unit and session purpose statements.
- To practice teaching according to plans we have prepared.

A Class Plan

1. Help class members understand that the brief time we have with students each week is multiplied as we share in a larger curriculum plan. Ask students what contribution and way of extending their outreach is furthered by each of the following elements in a curriculum plan, as described in the chapter:

a. A general objective.

b. A coordinated cycle of courses at many age levels.

c. Common annual or quarterly emphases.

d. A series of coordinated units.

e. Unit and session purposes.

f. Flexible but carefully prepared session plans.

2. Examine different types of unit and session purpose statements and discover the help they give to teaching. (Practice making a purpose statement tailored to individual classes.)

3. Examine the elements in step-by-step session development

and practice making individual session plans, adapting printed resource plans to local needs.

4. Where possible let students actually teach the plan they have prepared before concluding this course or observe another person teaching according to a session plan.

5. Evaluate the session taught or observed by the students.